Praise for *The Winner's Brain*

"*The Winner's Brain* is packed with fascinating stories of actions that can contribute to higher performance. Brown and Fenske translate the latest neuroscience research into practical tools for athletes, activists, or the average person."

—ROSABETH MOSS KANTER, Harvard Business
School Professor, Director of the Harvard
Advanced Leadership Initiative, and
author of *Confidence* and *SuperCorp*

"Whatever your goal: laser focus, mindful motivation, or seamless adaptability, *The Winner's Brain* offers accessible, thought-provoking, immediately-applicable strategies for success."

—FRANCES COLE JONES, author of *How to Wow*
and *The Wow Factor: The 33 Things You
Must (and Must Not) Do to Guarantee
Your Edge in Today's Business World*

"Brown and Fenske intertwine stories, studies and step-by-step tips to explain each of these strategies, talk about the science behind them and offer practical ways to develop them . . . They offer plenty of tools to help anyone develop habits to better achieve life goals." —*Los Angeles Times*

"If success is your desired destination, *The Winner's Brain* provides a useful road map." —*Energy Times*

"[Drs. Brown and Fenske] have described a set of strategies for remaining mentally sharp even under trying circumstances. In their book, *The Winner's Brain: 8 Strategies Great Minds Use to Achieve Success*, Drs. Brown and Fenske outline an approach they derive from well-known psychotherapies and discoveries in neuroscience. The strategies they suggest can be applied in the clinic, the classroom, and the workplace."

—Harvard Mental Health Letter

"Crisply written and backed by meticulously researched facts."

—Tucson Citizen

"If you are looking to unlock your own potential, you might want to start by reading this interesting book."

—Bookviews.com

"The book is filled with medical research, but also some great stories . . . With examinations of decision making, emotions, focus, memory, and more, *The Winner's Brain* helps us think differently about our potential and shows us how to act upon it."

—800 CEO Read

"Translate[s] cutting-edge neuroscience into a roadmap for training your brain to perform at a higher level and increasing your potential for success—however you define it."

—Taste for Life

"An informative read for those who want to better understand their own gray matter." *—ForeWord This Week*

The
Winner's
Brain

Jeff Brown AND Mark Fenske

WITH Liz Neporent

The Winners Brain

8 Strategies Great Minds Use to Achieve Success

Da Capo
∞
LIFE
LONG

A Member of the Perseus Books Group

Editorial production by *Marra*thon Production Services. www.marrathon.net
Design and production by Jane Raese
Text set in 12-point Bulmer

Cataloging-in-Publication Data for this book is available from the Library of Congress.
HC ISBN 978-0-7382-1360-6
PB ISBN 978-0-7382-1469-6

First Da Capo Press edition 2010
First Da Capo Press paperback edition 2011

Published by Da Capo Press
A Member of the Perseus Books Group
www.dacapopress.com

Note: The information in this book is true and complete to the best of our knowledge. This book is intended only as an informative guide for those wishing to know more about health issues. In no way is this book intended to replace, countermand, or conflict with the advice given to you by your own physician. The ultimate decision concerning care should be made between you and your doctor. We strongly recommend you follow his or her advice. Information in this book is general and is offered with no guarantees on the part of the authors or Da Capo Press. The authors and publisher disclaim all liability in connection with the use of this book.

Da Capo Press books are available at special discounts for bulk purchases in the U.S. by corporations, institutions, and other organizations. For more information, please contact the Special Markets Department at the Perseus Books Group, 2300 Chestnut Street, Suite 200, Philadelphia, PA, 19103, or call (800) 810-4145, ext. 5000, or e-mail special.markets@perseusbooks.com.

10 9 8 7 6 5 4 3 2 1

For Karen, Jake, and Nathan,
my very favorite group of Winners.

FROM JEFF

For Carolynne and Grant.
Brown Team Go!

FROM LIZ

In loving memory of my father,
Lewis Marshall Neporent, M.D.

Contents

CONTENTS

The
Winner's
Brain

PART ONE

Understanding the Winner's Brain

Introduction

PEOPLE WHO ARE SUCCESSFUL in life have one thing in common: They all seem to be doing something different and special with their neurocircuitry to maximize their potential and achieve their goals. We believe that's what gives these people a Winner's Brain.

The average brain does a pretty good job of getting by day to day. After all, it has over one hundred billion brain cells serviced by a super-highway of blood vessels to help you think your thoughts, move your body, and experience the world around you, acting with a combination of speed and efficiency that even the most advanced computers can't rival. But presumably you are reading this book because of a desire to move beyond just getting by. You want to excel in life and achieve the goals that matter to you most.

Maybe you're considering a career change or launching a new business, yet haven't had the wherewithal to take the leap. Maybe you feel stuck at work and are unclear how to get ahead. Perhaps you've lost your job and are searching for a better situation. Wherever you are in life, whatever your goals, you want to expand your limits and open up your possibilities.

Contrary to popular belief, high personal achievement has very little to do with your IQ, your life circumstances, your financial resources, knowing the right people, or even luck. Take, for example, the great

French sculptor Auguste Rodin, who came from a poor family and was rejected from art school three times. Despite butting up against constant rejection, he bounced back time and again, using each failure and disappointment as an opportunity to fuel his talents and his passions. As you shall see once you dive into the upcoming chapters, Resilience and Motivation are two of the critical abilities for which Winner's Brains are wired.

The Partnership of Brain and Behavior

Our combined expertise as a cognitive behavioral psychologist (Jeff) and a cognitive neuroscientist (Mark) places us in a unique position to explain how the cognitive mechanisms of the human brain are associated with success. We have seen from our respective work how the strategies shared in this book can influence thoughts and behavior and help individuals push past unpleasant life circumstances, allowing them to blossom and grow. Seeing people routinely rise above challenges—sometimes incredibly harsh ones—and consistently flourish is one of the primary reasons Jeff became so interested in the science of success. And we've also seen evidence that these same strategies can literally reshape the brain. Brains that perform successfully really do "light up" differently and work more efficiently, and Mark has investigated just how the structure and function of brains are altered as a result of how their owners use them.

Winner's Brains actually operate differently than the average brain. We know this, in part, because of technological advances that let us see individual differences in how neural areas light up on scans of brains as they spring into action. By measuring physiological changes related to neural activity, such as increases in blood flow within the brain, techniques such as fMRI (functional Magnetic Resonance Imaging) can help us see which areas of the brain are relatively more active and participating as a corresponding thought, emotion, or behavior is playing out. (If, for example, someone sneaks up behind you and yells "Boo!" that instant jolt of fear that surges through your body is associated with increased activity within the amygdala, an almond-shaped structure in the medial temporal lobe—the structure that's most closely associated with identifying threats and evaluating the possibility of harm.) We've found the following:

A Winner's Brain is very good at tuning out distractions and choosing the best way to focus on a task (there are different types of focus the brain is capable of) in order to get the best outcome. A study led by Daniel Weissman at the University of Michigan showed that participants were able to stop and reorient their brain's processing power to help them perform better despite interruptions. We call the deliberate form of this strategy *focus reinvestment.* With practice, this type of skill is something you can develop for yourself to reduce your own attention-related errors. Even if previous tries to change jobs, find a mate, or attain any other objective have failed in the past, an extra dose of focus may be just what you need to get you over the hump.

Winner's Brains seem to maintain a bottomless effort supply. A youngster who is forced to practice his piano lessons one hour every day, even if he doesn't want to and has no interest in playing, is unlikely to become an accomplished pianist. But a child who loves music, is interested in playing, and understands the potential of success will prioritize and complete her practice sessions—even at the end of her most tiring days. She is more likely to become a proficient, successful player because of her ability to sustain the effort.

Support for this idea comes from studies like one by Debra Gusnard and colleagues at Washington University School of Medicine, who measured people's brain activity while they viewed a random series of images that were either emotionally stimulating or dull. These people also filled out self-assessments regarding their day-to-day level of persistence in completing tasks. Subjects with high persistence scores showed, during periods of the experiment containing mostly dull images, increased activity in brain regions known to contribute to motivational drive. Subjects with low persistence scores showed *decreased* activity in these regions. Winner's Brains fire up Motivation to push through boredom, while brains of less tenacious individuals seem to run out of steam.

Winner's Brains adapt in exceptional ways over time, harnessing a process known as neuroplasticity. Every time you think a thought, feel an emotion, or execute a behavior, there is always some sort of corresponding change within your brain. In some instances we can detect these alterations in the brain's physical landscape. Later in this book, you'll read about London Black Cab drivers who have regions of the hippocampus—an area of the brain involved in memory and spatial navigation—that are considerably larger than that of the average person. Research by Eleanor Maguire and colleagues at University College London suggests that these cab drivers likely started out with fairly ordinary brains. But when motivated to commit routes to memory, they quite literally built a better brain, neuron by neuron. This is something virtually anyone should be able to do—including you—if you quite literally put your mind to it.

Many people view the brain as a mysterious, abstract structure—almost like a set of master controls that run on autopilot behind a locked door to which one has no real access. This simply isn't the case. You have the ability to unlock the door and consciously, deliberately, and successfully control much of your brain's switchboard in order to better position yourself to achieve your goals and dreams. The brain is active and subject to change no matter what you do—this is one of the key discoveries of modern neuroscience. What sets the owner of a Winner's Brain apart is the desire and the know-how to take charge of the process.

Our definition of Winners encompasses the usual conception: people who meet with extraordinary success in the particular aspects of life they value the most. Winners achieve what they set out to accomplish, whether they wish to master a golf swing, raise a confident child, or climb the corporate ladder. But we would add more: The kind of Winners we are talking about revel in the journey toward their goals almost as much as the destination itself, and they strive for the type of success that helps make the world a better place. And whether they realize it or not, virtually all Winners rely on the specific brain strategies we lay out in this book to come out on top.

Throughout this book, dozens of our Winners tell their stories, which illuminate the science and theories. They come from all walks of life: artists and inventors, musicians and business people, a high-altitude window washer, an Olympic champion. Many are well known, like blues great B. B. King, Olympic gold medalist Kerri Strug, actress Laura Linney, and motivational speaker Trisha Meili, the Central Park jogger. They all meet the definition of success in their own unique way. Our interviews reveal surprising, often touching, and enlightening information aimed at showing how anyone can change their thinking to improve their life.

To be clear, not everyone with a Winner's Brain walks around with a gold medal, an Oscar, or a million-dollar paycheck. Some of the people you'll meet consider their greatest accomplishment being a college graduate, a superb cab driver, or a working artist. They are every bit as amazing as the celebrities you will meet in this book because they have accomplished the things in life that are most important to them personally, often in the face of extreme adversity.

What It *Doesn't* Take

We'd also like to dispel the myth that achievers are all born hardwired for success, that you are either born with a high-functioning brain or you aren't. We know that the brain changes based on what its owner chooses to do with it. And yes, you do have a certain amount of control over the process. Many of the studies we present in this book demonstrate this cause and effect convincingly. What has emerged from this research and our representative interviews is that Winners are often forced to do some extensive rewiring so they can leap over life's obstacles and stay on the path to success. In addition, many didn't start with the vast financial resources or the important personal connections you might expect. And very few fit the definition of lucky. All of them demonstrate a strategic and proactive use of brain power—they take charge of their brain's Adaptability rather than leaving it to chance or waiting for the perfect set of circumstances to present themselves.

In the case of how your brain operates, nature does not always trump nurture: They work together. One of the central themes of this book is that there are many ways to shape your brain to more fully express its genetic potential. As you'll learn in the chapter on Adaptability, your brain's structure and functioning will continue to change over time even if you don't do anything strategic with it—just not necessarily the way you wish. So why not take the reins and nurture the nature you have? Even into old age, we all can adapt our brain. Indeed, one of the well-established laws of neuroscience is that the brain retains a capacity for change until the day you die. You are not enslaved by a brain that can only respond in one way. There are endless opportunities for improvement; and when you actively take charge of how your brain works, you have a better chance of influencing your fortunes.

Welcome to the Winner's Brain

A Winner's Brain employs definable strategies that allow it to operate more effectively. Many books about success take a purely behavioral approach but fail to tie the essential functions of the brain to specific behaviors. Yet the two are inextricably bound. How you think and behave will affect your brain, and changes in your brain can in turn further affect your thoughts and behavior.

Here's how the book is organized: Part One begins with a quick tour of the brain itself, followed by a brief history of modern neuroscience and how it has changed the way we look at both the brain and psychology today. Then we explain the neural mechanisms you will strive to develop in the process of your journey to success. We did an extensive review of existing research and drew from clinical experience to create a Winner's Profile that describes five different categories of cognitive skills, which we call BrainPower Tools. You might be born with a combination of some or all of these tools functioning to varying degrees, but as we explain, you can strengthen them all through the use of the cognitive strategies we detail in the second part of the book.

In the second part of the book, outlining our eight Win Factors, we explain how readers can perfect their individual profile by enhancing eight different traits that govern how the brain approaches a variety of tasks—everything from heightening Self-Awareness (Factor #1) to using the right type of Focus at the right time (Factor #3) to building a more effective Memory (Factor #5). Much of our advice is simple and easy to implement, though some of it requires a little elbow grease (or is it "neuron grease" in this case?) to put into action. Each strategy you adopt can help you perform at a higher level.

Finally, throughout the book, you'll see dozens of simple to-do's we call Brainstorms, identified by the symbol shown at right. These often surprising and unexpected tactics are based on scientific research and have been designed to boost the brain's winning capabilities. There are no gimmicky games, puzzles, or twisters here—and many of our Brainstorms can be adopted and applied almost immediately.

The beauty is that everyone has what it takes to be successful, quite simply because everyone has a brain. Even if you've never tried particularly hard to harness the power of your grey and white matter, you have the capacity to transform your thinking, emotions, behavior, and even the physical structure of your brain itself to reach your full potential. You own your brain; it's available for use 24/7, free of charge. Just as doing bicep curls will reshape and add inches to your arms, exercising with the strategies we detail on the following pages will help reshape, develop, and optimize the neurocognitive characteristics that are essential for success.

Image © Joe Cicak

One of the earliest casts of Rodin's great bronze statue *The Thinker* can be found in the gardens at the Musée Rodin in Paris. If you look closely at this famous muscular man perched deep in thought, you discover he is not a passive figure in any sense of the word. He leans forward, pressing his fist against his teeth and curling his toes around a rock, his entire body actively engaged in the effort of contemplation. He is powerful and full of intention. He's on the verge of putting his ideas into motion. As Rodin himself once remarked, "The fertile thought slowly elaborates itself within his brain. He is no longer a dreamer, he is a creator."

The Thinker is a perfect symbol for a book about how the human brain can be made your most valuable asset. Like *The Thinker* poised on the edge of a rock, you can proactively take charge of your mind, and in doing so, move from dreamer to creator, from someone who sits by and allows thoughts to wander to someone whose efforts and intentions translate into great ideas and decisive action. You can think your way to success.

You can become a Winner.

CHAPTER 1

A Quick Brain Tour

WHEN MOST PEOPLE THINK about their brain, they don't think about it as an actual physical structure. To many, the brain is an undefined grey mass that somehow warehouses memories and experiences and controls all of our actions. But this is like defining a country only by its gross domestic product, when, in fact, it is really comprised of states, counties, municipalities, job sectors, companies, and individual workers, all contributing to the overall financial health of the country.

The sophisticated anatomy of the brain includes many names, but if you are unfamiliar with them, rest assured that we will explain and define them simply and clearly. We mention over and over again a few brain structures that are critical Winner's Brain areas, so here's a cheat sheet to them.

Cerebral Cortex: It's what helps you experience the world around you—and reflect upon it later. Think of this folded, wrinkled outermost covering of the brain as the hamster on the wheel responsible for generating your brain's considerable computational power. Often referred to as grey matter (its specialized brain cells, aka neurons, lack the insulation that gives much of the rest of the brain its white color), the cortex is important for your ability to process and interact with the world around you. The

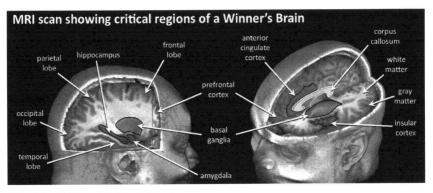

3D rendering of Jeff Brown's brain by Mark Fenske.

four lobes of the cortex each have broadly assigned, specialized functions: the **occipital lobe** (vision); the **temporal lobe** (hearing, language, memory, and object and scene recognition); the **parietal lobe** (somatosensory processing such as touch and temperature, visuospatial processing, attention, visually guided actions); and the **frontal lobe** (motor processing, working memory, decision making, and other higher mental functions).

The wiring underneath the cortex consists of neurons that are insulated to ensure speedy signaling. This *white matter* acts as the brain's switchboard, connecting the different cortical regions to each other and to the rest of the nervous system.

One of the most important bundles of white-matter fibers is the **corpus callosum**. It connects the **left and right hemispheres** of the brain that are separated by a deep groove, the longitudinal fissure, which runs straight down its middle. While each hemisphere contains essentially the same set of specialized neural structures, there tend to be some important differences between the two. The left hemisphere, for example, is a bit more involved with language and dealing with symbols, while the right hemisphere is predisposed to dealing with visual-spatial processing and recognizing faces, among other things. The corpus callosum bridges the gap, allowing the integration of information across hemispheres.

Prefrontal Cortex: Are you able to read this book while simultaneously keeping track of when to get off the bus and thinking about the emails you need to write once you get to work? This sort of mental multitasking involves the prefrontal cortex, a region associated with making decisions, forming goals, and planning how to accomplish them, as well as making predictions based on past experience and evaluating right from wrong. The forward-most part of the frontal lobe, this region also has critical influence on your personality and on proper behavior in social situations.

Anterior Cingulate Cortex (ACC): If you want a piece of cake while you're on a diet, the ACC helps to inform other brain structures, such as the prefrontal cortex, that there is a conflict to resolve. The ACC has many cognitive and emotion-related functions, but as it relates to a Winner's Brain, it's an area associated with detecting errors, balancing emotions, and making decisions. It resides near the front and center of the brain, right above the corpus callosum.

Insula: That wave of nausea you get when you get a whiff of sour milk is courtesy of the insula, a structure buried deep within the cerebral cortex between the temporal lobe and the parietal lobe. Its proper name is actually the insular cortex, and it's linked to perceiving and experiencing certain aspects of emotion, particularly physical and psychological revulsion, as well as perception and self-awareness of our internal bodily states.

Amygdala: This almond-shaped structure is found nestled within the medial temporal lobe on each side of the brain about two inches behind the eye. The amygdala is the structure most often associated with emotion, particularly emotionally charged memories that involve learning and responses, like touching a hot stove. If you're afraid of snakes or clowns, thank your amygdala, which appears to be the area most closely associated with identifying threats and evaluating the possibility of harm.

Hippocampus: The hippocampus is best known for its role in forming the sort of long-term memories that you can talk about and relate to others, like where you went on vacation last year or which short cut to take during rush hour. Also related to spatial navigation and memory, the hippocampus is useful in helping you successfully navigate a dark room you are familiar with. This structure resides within the medial temporal lobe; it's nestled directly behind the amygdala and gradually curves upward as it extends toward the back of the brain.

Basal Ganglia: Above the amygdala and hippocampus on each side of the brain lie a group of nuclei—compact clusters of neurons—which together are known as the basal ganglia. It is considered an important component of the brain's reward and motivational systems, and much of your get-up-and-go energy is channeled through there. It's in close communication with the cerebral cortex and, among other things, helps you perform well-practiced physical actions like tying your shoes and buttoning your shirt.

These are just the highlights, but don't forget: The entire brain works together in various ways to create Winning thoughts, emotions, and actions.

CHAPTER 2

The Amazing History of Modern Neuroscience

The Search for a Winning Formula

Modern neuroscience is built upon a strong foundation of individual discoveries, each of which has played its part in unraveling the mysteries of the brain and how it supports our thoughts and behavior. This foundation is critical for understanding how the brain works and identifying the specific factors involved in developing a Winner's Brain.

THE CHICAGO WORLD'S FAIR opened on May 27, 1933, forty years after the previous Chicago World's Fair, the Columbia Exposition of 1893, which had celebrated the 400th anniversary of Columbus's discovery of America. It was very much a science fair, and its lights and electricity were activated by rays from the star Arcturus, 40 light-years away. Visitors were awed by the towering dream city that rose up from what had been landfill and now stretched across the 427 acres of Burnham Park, on the shores of Lake Michigan. Though the fair was held in the depths of the Great Depression, more than 48 million people passed through its gates, gladly paying the 50 cents daily admission to witness the uncharted limits of human imagination and to feast upon all the information and experience the Great Fair had to offer.

The event was conceived as a tribute to science and technology, hence its moniker, "A Century of Progress." Its 400,000-square-foot Hall of Science included a miniature oil refinery, an exhibit on evolution, and a ten-foot-tall robot that explained digestion. On public display for one of the first times ever was a dazzling new invention called television.

And then there was the psychograph, which for just ten cents scanned a fairgoer's brain. This brain-scanning machine resembled an old-fashioned beauty salon hair dryer with dozens of long metal probes jutting from its helmet. The subject sat in a chair and the headpiece was

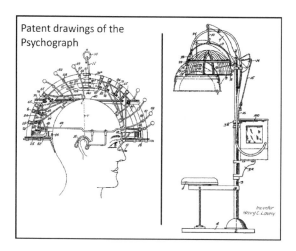

Patent drawings of the Psychograph

lowered and adjusted, then the operator pulled back a lever to activate the belt-driven motor, which sent out low-voltage signals meant to map the various regions, or what the psychograph read as "organs," of the brain. Once the examination was complete, an enormous dot matrix printer whirred into action, providing each client with a personal "neuroanalysis" titled "The Guide o' Life."

The psychograph was the mechanical counterpart of a then century-old practice known as phrenology, a mixture of brain science, psychology, and philosophy. Phrenologists believed that certain traits literally shaped the brain, and the brain responded by pushing and shifting against the skull, leaving telltale lumps and divots. To phrenologists, an individual's talent and character were easily readable if you knew how to correctly interpret the skull's topography; for example, the phrenological brain spot for musicality was located at the base of the temple, just above the left eye. The justification for this was found in paintings of Mozart, who was often depicted with his finger placed on that very spot when composing music.

Before the invention of the psychograph, phrenologists relied on a series of charts superimposed upon ink drawings and plaster models of skulls to make their case. But by the turn of the twentieth century, many of their theories had been largely discredited and were beginning to be supplanted by the burgeoning fields of psychology and neuroscience. By the time the machine made its appearance at the Chicago fair, both professionals and the general public alike had come to regard phrenology as more novelty act than science (this may be why the psychograph was banished from the Hall of Science and placed among the circus and carnival attractions on the Midway; the Temple of Phrenology exhibit lay sandwiched between Midget Village and the Ripley's Believe It or Not tent, just around the corner from the flea circus).

Yet phrenologists played an important, if misguided, role in the early advancement of modern neuroscience. They were attempting to unlock the secrets of personality and behavior by linking specific mind functions to size differences across the different areas of the brain. The phrenologists' notion that the brain was the seat of thought, emotion, and behavior was revolutionary compared to some historical viewpoints. The ancient Egyptians, for example, thought the heart was responsible for thought and higher functioning; they carefully preserved the heart and discarded the brain during the embalming process. And while subsequent scholars, such as the ancient Greek physician Alcmaeon, advanced the possibility that the brain was important for thought and perception, even notable thinkers such as Aristotle continued to believe that the heart was the most critical thought-related organ—indeed, he thought the brain acted primarily as a radiating device for cooling blood coming through the heart. These examples illustrate how mankind has been striving to understand the seat of intellect for millennia. The various and shifting points of view found along the way eventually settled squarely on the brain. We have been fascinated ever since by what makes this critical organ tick and by pondering how its power might be harnessed.

In this chapter, we highlight some of the critical points in the recent history of psychology and neuroscience, instances over the past 200 years that have helped advance our knowledge of the brain and how it works. Many of the cases from earlier days depended upon unhappy events where patients literally (and often unintentionally) gave their lives for the betterment of neuroscience when their brains were examined after accident or death. These sacrifices gave investigators a starting point for gaining knowledge about where memories are formed, which structures hold the key to moral behavior, how we process language, and so on. Every example we describe provides supporting evidence of how changing the brain changes how you think, feel or behave and how these changes can lead you to success.

In our search for what makes a Winner's Brain operate so effectively, our goals were not so different from those of the phrenologists. They invented the psychograph in an attempt to scan the brain. To them, the landscape of the skull was a window into the function of the specialized areas of the brain that lay beneath. With this book, we are pursuing the same goals, but with the knowledge that the skull is too hard and the brain too soft to give us answers in a topographical way. What you do with your brain causes it to grow and change—and this has been proven by examining the brain with the incredible tools we have available to us today. It is also demonstrated in the real world by people who do the things they want in life.

Brain Science with a Bang

The phrenologists' contention that specific structures in the brain might be specialized for different aspects of thought, emotion, and behavior was radical at the time and, to some extent, on the right track. Their influence can be seen front and center in one of the most pivotal cases from the history of brain study.

In the summer of 1848, Phineas P. Gage, a 25-year-old railroad construction foreman from Vermont, accidentally set off an explosion that sent an iron bar rocketing through the air. The bar entered his left cheek, pierced the base of his skull, traversed through the front of his brain, and exited at high speed through the top of his head before landing at least 100 feet away, covered with blood and bits of brain. Although Phineas recovered his senses shortly after the accident and witnesses reported he spoke rationally, they soon realized that "Gage was no longer Gage."

Previously he had been described as having a well-balanced mind and as someone who was persistent about executing all of his plans into action. Now he was rude, profane, and wildly inconsiderate, someone totally incapable of making good choices. Gage spent the rest of his days wandering aimlessly from one menial farm job to the next, even at one point displaying himself as an oddity in P. T. Barnum's Museum in New York City alongside bearded ladies and dwarfs. He carried the five-foot-long bar around with him until his death at the age of 38. Recently we were able to see the bar, along with Phineas Gage's skull, at the Warren Anatomical Museum, part of Harvard's Countway Library of Medicine in Boston.

Prominent phrenologists who reflected on Gage's case accurately attributed his changed personality to brain damage. Regardless of phrenology's shortcomings, its basic premise that different parts of the brain contribute to different traits and abilities correctly supported the conclusion that the blast had spared Gage's language and motor centers but not the parts of the brain responsible for character and reason. Given the location of the injury, it was one of the first solid clues that the prefrontal cortex, part of the frontal lobe of the brain, might actually contribute to basic traits like good judgment and social manners.

This fundamental truth about how such faculties are localized within the brain would take decades to prove. French scientist Paul Broca kept the ball rolling in 1861 by tracing language difficulties of stroke patients to damage in their brains' left frontal lobes, eventually attributing the master center of speech production to one square inch of grey matter rather than the lumpiness of a person's head. In his honor, this tiny patch of cerebral real estate was christened Broca's area.

Twelve years later, another European, the psychiatrist Carl Wernicke, connected a patient's inability to comprehend speech to damage within another area, the left temporal lobe. The temporal lobes can be found on each side of the bottom half of the brain, running from just behind the temples to just behind the ears. Beyond advancing the understanding of how the brain processes language, the possibility that the brain region involved in language comprehension was separate from that for language production helped scientists understand that a basic ability such as language was not confined to a single part of the brain. They were beginning to realize that different aspects of these fundamental abilities could arise in different regions of the brain. This meant that there had to be a lot of communication and coordinated effort going on between these different brain structures to support something as effortless as carrying on a conversation.

Living in the Moment

Not quite a century after Gage's meeting with the metal rod, another ill-fated soul unwittingly furthered the study of neuroscience. Henry Molaison, also known as Patient H.M. until his recent death, could recall the stock market crash of 1929 and the Chicago World's Fair, but not a recent stroll through the woods or a person he had met the day before. At the age of nine, H.M. fell off a bike and subsequently suffered from epileptic seizures until age 27, when a surgeon, in 1953, removed sections of his medial temporal lobes—parts closer to the middle of his brain—as a treatment. This did the trick for eliminating H.M.'s seizures—but consequently wiped out his ability to create new long-term memories. Thereafter he became the subject of intense scientific study; experts from all over the world came to assess him. But H.M. never seemed to mind. Actually, he never remembered any of it.

In the course of his epilepsy surgery, two-thirds of H.M.'s hippocampus—a curved structure within the medial temporal lobes—had been removed. Considering H.M. was then only able to recall experiences that happened before his operation, his surgeon, William Scoville, and neuropsychologist, Brenda Milner, concluded that a key function of the hippocampus is to form declarative memories, the type of memories you can actively reflect upon and talk about. But what Milner and subsequent investigators also found interesting is that many of H.M.'s other memory functions were preserved. In one experiment, H.M. was asked to trace a line between two outlines of a five-point star, one inside the other, while watching his hand and the star in a mirror, a difficult skill for anyone to master. Every time H.M. picked up the pencil, he experienced tracing the star as if it was the first time. Yet he gradually got very good at it.

This is because H.M.'s cerebellum, the fist-sized lump at the base and back of the brain, and his basal ganglia, nearer to the center of the brain, remained intact. These regions are key for what scientists call procedural memory, which enabled him to acquire new motor skills like tracing the star or solving a puzzle that required stacking disks in a specific order. However, lacking the ability to form conscious memories of new events, he could not explicitly recall ever having learned these skills. His short-term and working memory were also in good shape; he was able to memorize lists of words and hold information in his head for short periods of time about as well as the average person. But for the next 55 years, until his death in a Connecticut nursing home, you could say H.M. truly lived in the moment.

Like Gage before him, H.M.'s bad luck stands as one of the great milestones in the study of neuroscience. His selective memory function helped explain the link between the brain's structure and specific psychological processes. It was further proof of both the localized and holistic nature of the brain; that is, the brain has separate working parts that typically work together as a whole. The history of modern brain study is riddled with brain damage cases such as those of Gage and H.M. that have helped us, for example, link vision to the occipital lobes, attention and visual-spatial processing to the parietal lobes, and emotion to structures such as the amygdala. In these instances, things didn't work out so well for the individuals, but each stroke, knock on the head, and rod through the brain advanced our understanding of how this sophisticated organ works.

Moving Past Damage

Thankfully, we no longer have to wait for accidents to happen to examine the inner workings of the human mind. In fact, it was a few years before the Chicago fair in 1929 that a German psychiatrist, Hans Berger, was among the first to come up with a less invasive way to study the brain in action. He changed neuroscience forever in 1929 by attaching electrodes to his subjects' skulls to produce a graphic representation of the electrical activity of the brain. Berger watched these brain waves, as he called them, in a variety of different circumstances, charting how they shifted depending upon what a patient was doing or even thinking. If a patient sat quietly in a chair with his eyes closed, Berger noted slower alpha waves, and if the patient remained in the chair and opened his eyes, the brain switched to higher-frequency beta waves. In this way, Berger was able to assign the brain's electrical response to different types of attention and focus.

Refined forms of his electroencephalography (EEG) method are now used routinely in every hospital and neurologist's office. EEG and its cousin, MEG (magnetoencaphalography), which measures magnetic fields produced by electrical activity, both have millisecond-or-better temporal resolution. And so they are considered invaluable research tools for studying the timing of different brain functions as well as the general location from which they originate.

Since Berger, scientists have continued to devise ways of revealing the mysteries of the brain without having to wait for a patient to die. By 1970, Phineas Gage could have walked into any emergency room and undergone a simple battery of tests to reveal the damage to his *prefrontal cortex*, the part of the brain now known to be associated with complex cognitive behaviors, personality expression, decision making, and social behavior—precisely the traits that went south for Gage once the iron bar pierced his brain. Testing would not change the nature of the brain damage in a case as severe as Gage's, but at least doctors are able to determine the extent and effect of such an injury and how best to help the patient.

We now understand that the brain operates on many different levels. Besides plotting brain waves, we also learn about it by monitoring changes in blood flow and chemical interactions, and by observing how the different tissues and brain cells respond both in the moment and to repeated experiences. Some of the most common tools used in cognitive neuroscience research today are MRI (Magnetic Resonance Imaging) and the fMRI (functional Magnetic Resonance Imaging.)

During an MRI scan, a patient lies on a bed that slides into a large cylinder. The scanner's strong magnetic field forces the protons within the brain to line up much the same way metal filings line up under a magnet. Brief radio frequency pulses then push the protons out of alignment, causing them to emit a signal as they move back into place. How quickly they can move back into place, however, depends on the type of tissue in which the protons occur. The scanner picks up these differences and translates the contrasting signals into an anatomical map of the brain.

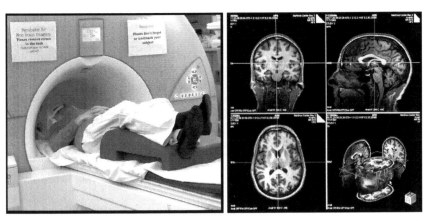

Liz Neporent inside an MRI scanner at the A.A. Martinos Center for Biomedical Imaging (left) and the resulting anatomical images of her brain (right). Photos by Cristine Lee.

An fMRI scan works much the same way, but instead of looking for difference in anatomy, it detects brain activity through relative changes in levels of blood oxygen. As active brain cells use up available oxygen, local increases in blood flow bring fresh red blood cells with iron-rich, oxygen-carrying hemoglobin. After releasing their oxygen, the iron atoms in hemoglobin produce small distortions in the surrounding magnetic field. Changes in the relative concentration of oxygen-carrying vs. oxygen-free hemoglobin therefore provide another set of contrasting signals that can be picked up by the scanner, which can be associated with differences in brain activity. With its focus on brain structure, MRI can measure differences in the thickness, density, and volume of different parts of the brain, whereas fMRI focuses on brain function, measuring levels of activity at thousands of points across the brain as it is actually happening.

While these are currently among the most widely used neuroimaging techniques, several other methods also provide critical data. Metabolic activity in the brain, for example, can be measured using a PET (positron emission tomography) scanner, while the brain's chemical makeup can be gauged using MRS (magnetic resonance spectroscopy). Meanwhile, carefully placed electrodes provide single-cell recordings, which can pinpoint the role of individual neurons in different brain functions, such as those involved in identifying your spouse, your child—or Brad Pitt. Researchers also continue to examine actual brain tissue, although they no longer have to rely on the unplanned sacrifice of people like Gage and H.M. Instead, people now willingly donate their brains upon their deaths to places like the Harvard Brain Tissue Resource Center at McLean Hospital in Belmont, Massachusetts, the largest brain bank in the world. Because most studies now require only a small sample of tissue, one brain can potentially support hundreds of projects.

All of these incredible techniques are the fruit of many decades of innovation and technological advances. Someday, the technology we describe in this chapter may allow us to gauge the effectiveness of cognitive strategies in real time, isolate and make changes at the cellular level, or even create new ways to maximize the brain. Right now, as we'll see throughout this book, these techniques can give us a glimpse of how a Winner's Brain operates.

The promise of this book lies in our current ability to identify areas in the brain associated with key cognitive elements connected to success, and to track new approaches that can lead to changes in how the brain operates. Recent advances in neuroimaging demonstrate that such approaches can lead to improvements in mental functions and that these improvements can cause changes in the physical structure of the brain itself. The extent of the positive changes made to the brain's structure partly reflects the durability of the corresponding improvements in the brain's ability to function. Such improvements can help you develop a Winner's Brain, and in the pages that follow we give examples of people who have improved themselves and done well in life using strategies that we describe in this book.

As Scott L. Rauch, M.D., chair of Partners Psychiatry and Mental Health and president and psychiatrist in chief of McLean Hospital, told us, "Modern brain imaging techniques have revolutionized neuroscience. In particular, in psychiatry, these methods have enabled investigators to safely explore the structure, function and chemical basis of psychiatric diseases as well as their treatments. Coupled with genetics, brain imaging approaches hold the greatest promise for [diagnosis and treatment]."

Scanning the Winner's Brain

In writing this book—and aiming to show how brain function relates to success—we've taken considerable care to avoid passing along erroneous or incomplete information. Each study we quote has been carefully considered, and in many cases we've spoken at length to the researchers who carried it out. We spoke to top thinkers in the fields of neuroscience and psychology, too, to avoid interpreting single studies in a vacuum and to ensure we have presented a comprehensive, cutting-edge view of how the brain works. We've also reinforced the findings by talking to people who personify a Winner's Brain. In almost every instance, we've been pleased to discover that what works in the lab often seems to lead to success in the real world, too. The people we interviewed throughout this book are living examples of winning ways of thinking, feeling, and behaving. They represent different professions, nationalities, and worldviews. With each study and interview, we have aimed to provide a better understanding of which traits—we call them Win Factors—make the greatest contributions to bettering the brain, along with deliberate strategies that are most likely to lead to positive changes in both brain and behavioral functioning.

Instead of simply reporting measurements from studies looking at the capacity of the brain, we've worked hard to uncover how that power helps someone become successful, and how you can harness it too. It makes sense that preserving and enhancing brain power by consciously trying to strengthen qualities like Memory and Emotional Balance (to name just two Win Factors) will increase your chances of achieving what's important to you.

As it turns out, optimizing your brain function is the key to feeling more satisfied, becoming more engaged in life, reaching your potential, and realizing your dreams. And the best part is, just about anyone can do it.

CHAPTER 3

BrainPower Tools

Five Essential Elements of Success

Winner's Brains have specific traits in common that we call BrainPower Tools. Some brains may possess some or all of these BrainPower Tools naturally—and if so, that's great—but we believe that almost anyone can enhance them by using the techniques in this book.

The Winner's Profile Quiz

Before you read this chapter, take this quick quiz to see if you currently have what it takes to set yourself up for success. This quiz isn't brain science per se, but it is derived from our experience and research associated with the psychological traits that appear to help people achieve and succeed. You were not born with these tools fully developed, but we believe it is possible to use your brain to strengthen them. As you will learn in this book, you can adapt the way your brain operates by consciously driving your thoughts, emotions, and behaviors in a specific direction.

To take the quiz, indicate how strongly you believe the statements or ideas below. Total your score by totaling up the numbers from all of your answers, then see how you measure up on the Winner's Brain continuum right now. After you've read through the chapters on the Win Factor strategies and given yourself at least a month to apply what you've learned, take the quiz again to see how your score changes. You may be surprised how your scores in your weaker areas have improved. You may find yourself responding in a more resilient way, staying more focused on the things you consider important or be better able to identify which talents are going to move you ahead in life.

Don't agree at all (1) *Somewhat agree (2)* *Completely agree (3)*

Goal Laser
1. Nothing ever distracts me from my goals. _____
2. I strive for my goals until I reach them—no matter what. _____
3. I always see a project through to the end. _____

Optimal Risk Gauge
4. I easily tolerate being outside of my comfort zone. _____
5. My decisions never lead to regret. _____
6. If something's too good to be true, then it usually is. _____

Talent Meter
7. If I'm not good at something, I find out how to improve. _____
8. I can accurately identify potential in others and myself. _____
9. It's easy for me to recognize what I don't know. _____

Opportunity Radar
10. I'm good at finding solutions when none seem to exist. _____
11. When something goes wrong, I try to see not the failure, but the opportunity in the setback. _____
12. When I try something and it doesn't work out the way I want it to, I reboot and find a new way to come at the problem. _____

Effort Accelerator
13. I can motivate myself easily. _____
14. I rarely procrastinate. _____
15. Even if I'm in last place, I find the strength to finish the race. _____

Score

45–40: You've got a head start; this book will help you put it all together. Your BrainPower Tools are well developed—now polish them to make them even stronger and more useful to you.

39–30: You're getting there but still have room for growth. You'll be a quick study. Some of your BrainPower Tools are operating smoothly, but others could use a bit of fine tuning. The strategies in this book are going to help you get to the next level.

29–20: You're just starting out, but you can get there. You have an awareness of your own potential. By taking on the brain-enhancing strategies we outline in this book, you will learn to direct your abilities to take you in the direction you want to go.

20 and below: Perhaps you thought you could never achieve success. You can. Like almost everyone, you have the raw materials it takes to get what you want from life, you just need some help developing the strategies and skills to get there.

As we began to write this book, it became remarkably clear how Winner's Brains tend to do many of the same things and operate in similar ways regardless of the direction their owners choose to take them. When we put our heads together to decide exactly what makes a Winner's Brain tick—Jeff in his capacity as a cognitive behavioral psychologist and Mark as a cognitive neuroscientist—the result was a profile consisting of eight Win Factors (more on those in a bit) that contribute to five different areas that we call BrainPower Tools: your Opportunity Radar, Optimal Risk Gauge, Goal Laser, Effort Accelerator, and Talent Meter.

How did we pinpoint these? First, we spent a lot of time reviewing how extraordinary brains operate differently in the moment and how they reshape themselves over time in response to the way they are used. From that emerged a picture of how Winners tend to use their brains to achieve success. Next, we discussed both our findings and our conclusions with some of the world's most respected experts in the various branches of neuroscience and psychology to confirm and refine our interpretation of the research. Speaking to top minds in the field helped us confidently reach conclusions that the research can actually support.

Finally, we wanted to illustrate how what is true in the lab can also be translated into real-life success. That's where the interviews come in with dozens of people we consider to be Winners. Every Winner in this book not only had to be successful in the area of their choosing, they had to clearly demonstrate the use of the BrainPower Tools and the Win Factor strategies we outline. In addition, no one featured here is to the manor born or has been handed anything without having to work hard and smart to get it. It was both gratifying and amazing to see how well the neuroscience and psychology match up to what actually helps people get what they want out of life.

We also concluded that some people quickly emerge with each Brain-Power Tool firing on all cylinders. They may not always realize they are using their brains in this way, but research indicates they are. Some of the studies we detail in this book start out by identifying people who already have the ability to do something well, then go on to examine how others might learn the particular strategy or trait. Other studies teach the success strategy and then look to neuroscience and psychology to explain how it works. Both types of studies are useful because they emphasize the average person's ability to move his or her brain in the direction of Winner.

So let's start by looking at each of the five BrainPower Tools and how they align with a Winner's Brain. In the process, you'll meet some of the Winners you'll learn more about later on and you'll get a taste of the science of success.

Tool #1: Opportunity Radar

No one can mistake Phyllis Diller's deep, staccato laugh for anyone's but hers. Hearing that signature cackle, you might think it's all been fun and games, but remember, she started out in the 1950s, an era that didn't exactly embrace female comics with open arms (unless you were Lucille Ball). Yet even with all of the challenges she faced as a young comedian, she would often pass up higher-paying gigs for ones that paid zilch as long as she thought it would allow her to do the act she wanted to do and be seen by the people she wanted to be seen by. That's a pretty gutsy move for someone who was barely making ends meet.

Like many of the Winners you'll meet throughout this book, Diller has the head (plus the hair!) for putting herself in the right place at the right time. We call this almost magical ability to spot a hot prospect *Opportunity Radar.*

Winners are continually scanning for blips on life's radar screen, and when a blip looks interesting, they investigate. Another great example is George de Mestral, the Swiss engineer who invented Velcro after examining the mountain thistle burrs he removed from his dog's fur. How many millions of people before de Mestral treated those burrs as nothing but a nuisance? People with exceptional Opportunity Radar recognize that opportunities don't always come gift-wrapped; more often than not, they come wrapped in a problem or an idea that everyone else has simply missed. This is a skill that serves everyone well. If a project you are working on bombs, you may not be thrilled, but if you can seize upon the things you learned along the way, perhaps there is one aspect you can develop into something great.

Recent research shows that people like Diller and de Mestral rely on what some have called the brain's promotion system, the aspects of the brain that are primed to search for and recognize a good opportunity. A team of researchers led by William Cunningham, for example, measured activity in emotion-related brain regions on an fMRI scanner, such as the amygdala and anterior cingulate, as individuals experienced emotionally positive and negative words. They found that the emotion-related regions were more sensitive to positive information in individuals who tend to seek advancement and accomplishment and were more reactive to negative information in those who tend to be more concerned with safety and responsibility. In addition to their ability to hone in on what may be potentially good, Winners may often depend on what most of us describe as intuition; however, digging a little deeper, we see that intuition is another aspect of Opportunity Radar that is stoked by an openness to view things with a fresh eye. This is why Diller was always able to spark new life into topics as well-worn as mothers-in-law and lazy husbands.

Was every career choice Diller made a good one? There's that famous laugh again as she admits to her share of face plants. You see, even the most winning of Winners will occasionally misread the blips on the Opportunity Radar screen. But having a keen radar helps stack the odds in your favor by helping you anticipate which opportunities may lead to success and which won't. You learn to avoid mistakes by slowing down and taking the time to assess the pros and cons of each opportunity. And when you stumble, your skin grows thicker with the confidence to carry on until the next good option comes along.

Tool #2: Optimal Risk Gauge

When Stephen Harris flashes that killer smile, right away most women think: Rock Star. Harris was a boy from a small working-class Welsh town who made it big in the 1980s playing bass for bands such as The Cult and Guns N' Roses—until he walked away from the scene to pursue other interests like painting and rock climbing. In September 2001, Harris had a life-changing epiphany after witnessing firsthand the pain and suffering following the terrorist attacks on the World Trade Center in New York City. Although he was never an enthusiastic student, he decided to go back to school and become a doctor. So at the age of 36, Harris took the risk and walked away from a comfortable existence to travel down a road where he won't officially pick up a stethoscope until he's 45. In the end, he says, taking the leap was an easy decision. He shrugs his shoulders when he points out that he would eventually be 45 in any case, so the greater risk would be looking back and realizing he hadn't pursued his dream. How many times have you wanted to take a leap but weren't sure how to evaluate the consequences?

People like Harris dovetail their Opportunity Radars with the Brain-Power Tool we call *Optimal Risk Gauge.* The sorts of risk taking they consider important don't involve betting your life savings on a horse race or highly speculative investments, nor are they casual risks like buying a lottery ticket or playing penny poker with the gang. For your Risk Gauge to be effective, you must be good at recognizing what the risks are, determine how much risk you can tolerate and whether or not you are willing and able to pay the consequences if you fail. You don't want to crash and burn from taking the plunge too often, but you do want to aim for a high enough payoff to make it worth your while.

Winners also try to better their situation (and sometimes the world) by taking risks that are substantial enough that they have a personal stake in the outcome, yet more gratifying than if they sat on the sidelines playing it safe. This is because lightweight goals aren't rewarding and insurmountable ones are a waste of time.

Evidence for this came in 2007 when Sabrina Tom and colleagues at the University of California, Los Angeles conducted a neuroeconomics experiment to see how the brain evaluates risk. Brain scans of 16 people who had a 50/50 chance of winning a bet for a small amount of cash showed that a broad set of regions associated with reward lit up as the potential gains increased—but those same areas dimmed as potential losses increased. Individuals with more pronounced levels of this neural "loss aversion" in regions such as the prefrontal cortex and ventral striatum (part of the basal ganglia) also tended to be those whose behavior showed greater sensitivity to potential losses. Winners like Harris are particularly good at calibrating this type of risk threshold to decide whether or not there is a chance worth taking. They know when to dive in headfirst and when to walk away.

Tool #3: Goal Laser

Iranian-born Ramin Karimloo first saw Andrew Lloyd Webber's musical *The Phantom of the Opera* at age 12, and he was hooked. Now, as he hurries into makeup before a night's performance in London's West End production of *Phantom*, you can tell he is just as excited and enthusiastic as that first moment he decided that playing the Phantom is what he wanted to do with his life.

Talk about follow-through! Karimloo has an impressive *Goal Laser*, the BrainPower Tool that helps you take aim at what you want out of life without allowing the static of distractions and stressors to interfere. It gives you the patience to delay gratification, often for years, without getting sidetracked along the way. Karimloo, for example, started by honing his skills singing in rock bands, then took parts in regional theater, eventually graduating to national touring companies. By his early twenties he was getting understudy roles on the London stage in hits such as *Les Misérables* and *Miss Saigon*. Finally, two weeks before his 25th birthday, he was awarded the lead role as the Phantom at London's Her Majesty's Theatre, where he continued until he left to prepare for his role as the main character in the premiere of *Love Never Dies*, the much-anticipated sequel to *Phantom*. (He was hand-picked for the role by Andrew Lloyd Webber himself.)

As studies show, people who have highly focused Goal Lasers like Karimloo tend to outperform their less self-directed peers because they intentionally and deliberately take steps to accomplish the things that are important to them. For example, a 2007 study of 223 salespeople by University of Texas at Arlington's Fernando Jaramillo and his colleagues found that the go-getters—those who showed the greatest amount of initiative—had an easier time translating their goals into actions compared to peers who had trouble taking initiative. So Goal Laser is about more than just having hopes and dreams; it's about locking on to them for as long as it takes to achieve them.

Tool #4: Effort Accelerator

Olympic gold medalist Kerri Strug is living proof of how valuable it is to have a strong *Effort Accelerator,* as we call the BrainPower Tool that supplies the push needed to keep on rolling over obstacles and sidestepping distractions as you march steadily toward achievement. As anyone who has ever tried to get in shape before knows, going to the gym day after day, year after year, and enduring hours of practice and physical punishment, as Strug did leading up to her heroic vault in the 1996 Summer Olympics, takes an incredible work ethic that goes well beyond simple motivation. There were certainly days where Strug wasn't particularly pumped up about what she had to do. But she did it. And she did it steadily, reliably, consistently. When she shares her lifelong motto "Never put off until tomorrow what you can do today," you can almost hear her revving up her Effort Accelerator.

The truth is, there are plenty of people who enjoy success when they aren't particularly motivated, but they seem to have the sort of self-directed energy inherent to the Effort Accelerator that keeps them chugging along. We see this in studies, such as that led by Debra Gusnard, where subjects who score high on the persistence scale (and show a lot of activity in the brain regions associated with motivational drive) are able to perform well even when tasks are boring and *unmotivating.* Comparatively, low-persistence individuals show decreased activity in those same regions when faced with such tasks.

This provides insight into Winners like Strug who use Motivation as the fuel in the tank and Effort Accelerator as the foot that presses down firmly on the gas pedal. Research has shown that the neurotransmitter dopamine plays a key role in providing this corresponding "urge to do something" through a key neural pathway joining structures in the midbrain and the ventral striatum. These regions kick into gear to move you from intention into action. In a recent fMRI study, Kari Eddington and colleagues at Duke University found that these brain areas are highly active when someone feels very motivated and action-oriented about a specific goal.

Tool #5: Talent Meter

Neuroimaging studies demonstrate how important a highly developed prefrontal cortex is for helping high achievers in a variety of fields gauge their own competence. Among other things, the medial aspect of this brain region contributes strongly to their *Talent Meter,* the BrainPower Tool that gives you a sense of what you're good at and what you're not.

One top LPGA golfer's Talent Meter kicked into high gear at a young age. Golfing didn't immediately emerge as her top gift—it was soccer then—but even as a preteen she had enough insight about herself to realize her destiny was on the links. Actually she excelled at a lot of things, both physically and academically, but her Talent Meter did a good job of divining the most successful path for her to take. It continues to guide her as she transitions from professional golf to other pursuits. Neuroimaging studies, such as a 2007 investigation led in Belgium by Arnaud D'Argembeau, suggest that a forward-most region of the medial prefrontal cortex is particularly important in helping a person reflect on their traits and abilities versus those of others. Such self-awareness is critical for maintaining a properly calibrated Talent Meter.

Indeed, having a well-calibrated Talent Meter is probably as important as possessing the actual talent itself. You might have the potential of becoming a great public speaker, an amazing parent, or an incredible teacher, but if you don't recognize those abilities within yourself you won't take the time to develop those natural talents. And all the hard work in the world won't turn you into a master chef if that sort of endeavor doesn't play to your strengths.

A finely tuned Talent Meter means being aware of weaknesses, too. The golf champion says she is brutally honest with herself; whether she is learning a new shot or now dipping a toe into the clothing business, she assesses what she knows and doesn't know. When she identifies a weakness, she is knowingly fanatical about learning as much as she can to minimize it. In this way she usually avoids the sand trap, so to speak, that many other people fall into when they judge themselves good at things, at which they in fact aren't.

This is what scientists have dubbed "the double whammy of incompetence"—and it can get you into trouble if you're not careful. Work by researchers such as Justin Kruger and David Dunning of Cornell University suggests that if you don't even realize you have gaps in your abilities, it may never occur to you to try and make improvements. Like everyone else, even great talents have opportunities for improvement.

All five BrainPower Tools are interrelated. We found this to be true over and over in both the studies we reviewed and on the stage of real life where Winners strut their stuff. And, while we believe it is possible to meet with some success with only a partial list of BrainPower Tools in your belt, we think you are more apt to achieve the things you want to in life when all of your bases are covered. Since everyone seems to be blessed with the capacity to strengthen every single tool to at least some degree—and often to a large degree—we don't see any reason why you shouldn't try. In doing so you are likely to meet with even more success.

The good news is there are strategies you can use to strengthen your BrainPower Tools, and they fall into one of eight general categories we call Win Factors. Each group of Win Factors addresses particular networks of brain regions to help make them operate more effectively. When you actively develop these on a consistent basis, your BrainPower Tools will take hold and become the overriding traits your brain displays in your everyday life. As a result, you are more likely to engage in activities that lead to success. You'll learn about these eight Winner's Brain strategies in detail in the next section of this book, but in short, they are:

Win Factor #1: Self-Awareness

A well-developed sense of Self-Awareness makes you more effective in your relationships, your job, and every other aspect of your life. When you take it to the level of a Winner's Brain, you are not only aware of how you relate to the rest of the world but also how the rest of the world relates to you. For some people, the fact that Self-Awareness is a skill to develop is surprising, but a number of recent studies show how it is possible and how much of a difference it makes when you do. Get ready to know yourself better.

Win Factor #2: Motivation

Though it may seem like Motivation is something that hits you like a bolt of lightning, research suggests that it flows through you like the phases of an electrical current. In a Winner's Brain, Motivation allows the individual to glide right over obstacles that often stop less determined people cold. It helps them push through challenges even when there is little external impetus to spur it on. Motivation primes the brain to see rewards even when they are a long way off and, indeed, even when there are no guarantees those rewards will ever come.

Win Factor #3: Focus

Emails! Phone calls! Instant messages! The brain is faced with a zoo of distractions that compete for our attention on a nearly constant basis. Winner's Brains have the ability to focus on tasks and activities in the moment, especially when the moment is also full of stressors and distractions. They deliberately calibrate their level of Focus under a wide variety of circumstances and can call on the best type of Focus for the task at hand.

Win Factor #4: Emotional Balance

The word "emotions" carries a negative connotation for some people, as if they're something to be avoided or they represent weakness. In fact, emotional responses are an important source of information that can have powerful effects on our decisions and behavior. When emotions are in balance, you can make them work in your favor and put feelings to good use rather than being driven blindly by them. As the research suggests, getting a handle on the aspects of the brain that control emotion will help you be more mindful of your feelings and allow you to channel them in productive ways—and we'll teach you how.

Win Factor #5: Memory

Winners don't just rely on Memory to help recollect Sunday dinners from long ago. It is most productive and useful when it's called upon to help anticipate the future and make predictions about the best way to respond to a novel situation. Individuals with a Winner's Brain excel at rapidly scanning their minds for old information that can help them anticipate and better understand novel circumstances. Winners can also recognize what they don't know and have mechanisms in place for uncovering that information quickly and accurately so they can integrate it and perform better.

Win Factor #6: Resilience

A common misconception is that past failures are an accurate representation of the future. Winners understand and embrace the importance of failing and, simply put, they get up at least one more time than anyone else. It's this act of "getting up"—be it mental or physical—that equals bounce, our term for Resilience. The resilient brain is about the big comeback and about not backing down.

Win Factor #7: Adaptability

The brain is surprisingly plastic and pliable. Winners embrace this fact. They take advantage of the fact that the brain keeps on changing no matter what and that the shape it takes will be directly molded by how they use it. This Adaptability is not confined to one region of the brain; it applies to areas throughout the brain. Any change to a thought, behavior, or emotion causes the brain to adapt even if the difference can't be immediately seen in brain scans. More substantial physical changes to the brain may come as the result of hard, conscious work, but even making small adjustments can alter how your brain responds. This is the foundation of every single Winner's Brain strategy and tip we offer.

Win Factor #8: Brain Care

Just because you can't see it stretching or flexing its muscles doesn't mean your brain doesn't do these things—at least metaphorically. Winners take good care of their brains. They feed it the right foods, give it plenty of sleep, and exercise it, just as they would their abs or their pecs. Like every other part of your body, how you treat your brain is how it will operate. And when you handle your brain with care, you are on your way to having a Winner's Brain.

PART TWO

Developing Your Winner's Brain

Self-Awareness

Thinking About Yourself
to Become a Winner

SELF-AWARENESS

An attuned sense of Self-Awareness will help you gain a better understanding of yourself, how you relate to the rest of the world, and how the rest of the world relates to you. By becoming more self-aware, you gain insight into why things happen to you the way they do—and how you can increase the chances of creating circumstances favorable to success.

Boost Your BrainPower: Self-Awareness especially raises your *Talent Meter* by helping you understand your talents and the limitations you need to overcome and improve upon. It is also a large part of *Effort Accelerator;* when you have a sense of what motivates you, you tend to choose the activities that keep you going.

LEONARDO BRINGS HIS HAND UP to his chin as he ponders two boxes that sit on a table in front of him. Jesse, the adult, asks him, "Leo, can you find the box Big Bird is under?"

Leo thinks for a moment and then shyly points to the small box. He's correct, so Jesse asks him another question. "Leo, can you find where *I* think Big Bird is?"

He points to the small box for the second time. Right again.

Jesse leaves the room but quickly returns, hunched over, with a hood pulled over his face so Leo won't recognize him. Leo watches as this hooded stranger takes Big Bird out from under the small box and places him under the big box. Jesse then creeps away, only to return a few seconds later with his hood off so Leo knows who he is.

Now he asks the same question again. "Leo, can you find where *I* think Big Bird is?"

No hesitation. Leo correctly points to the small box. As far as Leo is concerned, Jesse does not know about the switch and will assume that Big Bird is in the last place he saw him before he left the room. This ability to grasp that someone else might believe something you know to be untrue (what's known in psychology as the "false-belief test") is considered a major developmental milestone for children—and so too, for robots like Leo.

Human Nature

If Yoda had a pet it would look like Leo. His expressive eyes, kitten mouth, and soft rabbit ears convey a worldly wisdom and calm patience. But pulling back the curtain on Leo's cute and fuzzy exterior exposes a tangle of wires, circuit boards, and computers that endow him with the capacity to imagine himself in another person's shoes. Jesse is Jesse Gray, who, along with Matt Berlin and Cynthia Breazeal of the personal robotics lab at the Massachusetts Institute of Technology, is one of Leo's creators.

When we spoke to Jesse's colleague Matt Berlin about the "lost toy experiment" he helped design to test out Leo's abilities, he wanted to make sure we understood that the results are more than just a cute party game. "Leo is the world's most socially intelligent robot," he explained. "He possesses some of the same capabilities that humans have evolved to interact with one another: eye contact, gaze direction, turn-taking, shared attention—and in the case of the missing toy challenge, the ability to model the belief states of other people."

Accomplishing these comparatively simple cognitive and emotional tasks involves a mesh of software programmed to learn the way humans learn: by starting with a core of basic drives and abilities, then adding to them as physical and social experiences accrue. Whenever Leo meets someone new, he continues to process information about what he sees and experiences for himself. At the same time, he begins filing information from the other person's point of view, omitting on their behalf anything they are not aware of. As we saw, he's able to follow Big Bird's changing location while simultaneously keeping track of what Jesse Gray has or hasn't personally experienced.

"Our goal is to design robots that interact well with humans and are better team members," Berlin explains. "This is built around the idea that you can use the self as a simulator for understanding others."

Although Berlin is speaking about robots, he essentially echoes our Winner's Brain factor of Self-Awareness: It's the ability to "know thyself," especially as you relate to the rest of the world. We believe that a well-developed sense of Self-Awareness allows you to take advantage of your Talent Meter and better understand your limitations while shaping decisions in the moment and planning for the future. By giving you purpose and direction, strong Self-Awareness helps you to become more effective in your relationships, your job, and every other aspect of your life. This is why ancient Greek philosophers extolled Self-Awareness as the secret to comprehending human nature and why many modern day psychologists view it as an important goal in psychotherapy. It is also why Berlin is working so hard to achieve this in technologically advanced robots.

Mirror Neurons

From a purely neuroscientific standpoint, many researchers believe that the ability to walk a mile in your *own* shoes is related to a network of specialized neurons known as *mirror neurons,* originally discovered in Giacomo Rizzolatti's primate lab in Italy. They're so named for their apparent purpose of enabling you to imitate and reflect upon the behaviors and emotions you witness in others. In effect, observing another person's emotions activates your emotion.

Interestingly, mirror neurons may have originally evolved to enhance social awareness (how you perceive your place within a group), which was already beginning to establish itself within the brain. Mirror neurons for emotional states, which may exist in the anterior insula, anterior cingulate cortex, and inferior frontal cortex, may allow you to "feel" the experience of another person, then consider your own values and standards when evaluating the person's behavior. For example, if you readily recognize and empathize with the annoyance someone else feels after stubbing a toe, you are more likely to offer sympathy and assistance.

But as a bonus, you're more likely to avoid your own future toe stubbings. In essence, in the course of enhancing social awareness, mirror neurons may also help to increase Self-Awareness. These mutual increases in social and Self-Awareness work together so you have smoother interactions with people and the world around you in general—and in this case, fewer swollen toes.

Beyond mirror neurons, Self-Awareness appears to rely on a sprawling network of brain regions, rather than a single "me spot". Recent work by researchers such as Georg Northoff suggests that this network may be centered around a group of cortical structures running down the middle of the brain. These cortical midline structures appear to be involved in a host of Self-Awareness responsibilities, including recognizing the difference between yourself and others, monitoring and evaluating personal behavior, and recalling autobiographical history.

The insular cortex, nestled between of the fissures of the frontal, temporal, and parietal lobes, is another brain region that appears to be critical for Self-Awareness, even beyond its potential role mirroring the emotional states of others. The insula is already quite busy with other Winner's Brain activities, including some of those related to our own emotional states. These duties also include particularly important operations that help us track changes in internal bodily states and physical sensations—if you have an itch, the insula helps inform you about it and recruits other areas involved in helping you scratch it.

Somehow, in ways we are just beginning to understand, the cross-talk between different neural networks imbues you with a singularity of self. Winner's Brains in particular have a gift for harnessing this attribute, especially as it relates to your interactions with others and understanding the contributions you are able to make to the world. And, while Berlin admits that programming true Self-Awareness into robots has proven more challenging than expected, most humans have a wonderful capacity for the trait. Given the right information and a dash of practice, most of us can raise our Self-Awareness up to Winner's Brain levels.

Winners Are Authentic

When we interviewed Laura Linney for this book, she admitted in one of her responses, in a sweetly unassuming way, that she is "somewhat famous and recognizable." This, of course, is like saying fire is "somewhat hot." She has had major roles on the stage, in such films as *The Truman Show, Mystic River,* and *The Squid and the Whale,* and as Abigail Adams in the HBO mini-series *John Adams,* gleaning her an Emmy, a Golden Globe, three Oscar nominations, and two Tony nominations. She's constantly in the spotlight thanks to movies, TV, and other media and many people don't just know who she is—they feel like they know her.

"There was a moment a few years ago when I was going through a divorce and I was having a very tough day," she told us. "I was going to work on the subway and this very nice girl came up to me, but she was inappropriately excited to see me. I was clearly shut down in my world of iPod but she wanted my attention. I was as nice as I could be and I said hello, but I didn't continue the conversation and went back to my iPod. When I got off the subway I turned around to look back and realized she was in tears.

"It was very weird for me. In some ways I felt terrible. I didn't think I had been rude. But I realized I had way too much power and I resented it terribly. When I think about that moment, I still feel very uncomfortable."

As Linney will attest, celebrity can blur the line between your "public" self, the person we present to the rest of the world, and your "real" self, the person we are in private when the door is closed and no one else is watching. All of us maintain a public persona to a certain extent: Who hasn't put on a happy face at a party even after having a bad day? But for people who possess a highly evolved sense of Self-Awareness, these two selves are very close to the same thing, or at the very least there is a conscious awareness of how (and why) they are different. When you narrow the gap between your public and real self, it is easier to read how others experience you. You come across as unafraid to share your real self and are more likely to be perceived as a confident, authentic person. Likewise, you'll assess your personal interactions more accurately: A salesperson who is a good judge of his customers and comes across as a genuine person will probably sell more; a job applicant who presents herself honestly and correctly judges the reactions to her responses during an interview is more likely to get the job.

Most of us don't have to worry, as Linney does, that a bad mood or a bad hair day will wind up as a viral online video, which is why it's all the more admirable she seems to juggle her public versus her real self with a Winner's Brain. She recognizes that her fame can sometimes make others feel bad when she doesn't respond the way they want her to—even when her intentions are good and her actions are appropriate. She empathizes but also keeps it in perspective, realizing that she isn't as perfect as others may expect her to be. Housed within her cortical midline structures, the evaluation processes for both self-perception and sensitivity to others are presumably humming along nicely. And as studies show, good self-evaluators like Linney have a knack for using the frontal gyrus to carry on an inner dialog that helps them deal with the emotional aspects of a situation and behave in a way that tracks with her personal values.

The one caveat to this discussion is that there are times when what you put out there for all to see won't match your real self, and that's OK. There are certain things you may want to keep private and should. Perhaps it's best to share the details of your impending divorce or your financial troubles only with those closest to you. As you'll learn in the Resilience chapter, negative life experiences can sometimes lead to good outcomes. However, the details of those experiences may be painful. A Winner's Brain with an accurate sense of self recognizes healthy boundaries and knows when to be an open book—and when to close it up and put it on the shelf. Winners know the power of sharing themselves appropriately and where to draw that line.

Who Do You Think You Are?

Think you are perceptive about the difference between your public and real self? Answer these nine questions about yourself on a piece of paper, then ask a trusted friend to also answer them as they pertain to you. If both sets of answers match up pretty closely, then you probably have a good sense of who you are and how others experience you. If a noticeable discrepancy exists between your friend's answers and yours, then you may not have a clear, accurate understanding of how you impact those around you with your words, actions, and attitudes. Winner's Brains are constantly striving to understand themselves, so it's fine for you to ask your friend for more feedback.

1. Would you trust me with a secret?

2. Could you call me if you had an emergency?

3. What's the strongest factor that makes me a good friend?

4. Do you think I easily forgive people or am I a grudge holder?

5. What does my nonverbal language say to others?

6. Am I an optimist or a pessimist?

7. What do you get tired of me talking about?

8. What do you notice that I do when I'm feeling uncomfortable or nervous?

9. What one word do you think describes me best?

Body Language: Your Slip Is Showing

One of the goals of developing Winner's Brain Self-Awareness is to reduce the discrepancy between the real you and the public you, so it's important to know if you are generally successful at doing so. One way you can tell is by paying attention to more than just what people say. It takes you perhaps three seconds to verbally express how happy you are, but computational modeling and analysis of EEG data by Philippe Schyns and his University of Glasgow colleagues recently demonstrated that the brain typically requires less than 200 milliseconds to gather most of the information it needs from a facial expression to determine a person's true emotional state.

We collect volumes of information about the way people respond to us from a cocktail of nonverbal facial expressions and body language. Some of this information is clear and obvious. Lowered eyebrows, a wrinkled forehead, tensed eyelids, and tensed lips, for example, are universally understood to signify anger. (There are half a dozen of these universal facial expressions and perhaps a couple dozen more that would be recognized by people in most but not all cultures.)

Other hints about what a person is feeling leak out through fleeting micro-expressions that occur between or during intentional expression. These go by in a flash—so fast, very few of us consciously register them and so fast, even the person exhibiting the micro-expression is unaware of them and unable to control them. The modeling done in the Glasgow study suggests that the brain starts "scanning" for these expressions by looking at the other person's eyes, then zooming out to process the whole face, before zooming back in to examine specific diagnostic features, such as eyes open wide in fear, or a smiling mouth. It does all this in less time than it takes to blink an eye.

Nonverbal cues often convey emotions and ideas more powerfully than words perhaps because we learn how to read them as infants, long before we can speak or even understand speech. And after we learn to use words, things like posture, gesture, and face movement still manage to grab hold of the brain's right hemisphere and tell the story the person is trying to convey, either consciously or subconsciously. Interpreting nonverbal communication correctly is an important skill for improving Self-Awareness. Such cues transcend words and inform you of what someone else is really feeling about you. Winner's Brains take that information about the person's experience and respond in a way that enhances the relationship, maintaining authenticity along the way, which in turn gives you feedback about how that person experiences you.

Excellent actors know this and are careful students of nonverbal communication. Anyone can recite a dialogue, but what shapes a great performance are the nuances of expression and physicality. They telegraph important details about a character's personality, life experiences, and emotions to the audience in a way mere words cannot. When Linney was developing her character Abigail Adams, for the critically acclaimed HBO miniseries *John Adams,* she told us this was something she thought a lot about.

"There's not much known about her but I found in one biography . . . a footnote with the small detail that she was pigeon-toed. And just knowing that changed how I portrayed her. There was something about a pigeon-toed person and what that does to the body when you're corseted in all of that stiff clothing. It said something to me and it affected how I portrayed her, especially vocally."

Successful Self-Awareness, Past, Present, and Future

Winner's Brains are very good at traveling back in time to connect past sense of Self-Awareness with sense of self in the here and now. Years before the bright and articulate Elizabeth Hudson became a stay-at-home mom in a Calgary suburb, she spent two harrowing years on the streets

Read My Lips

From Dr. Jeff Brown: Here's a technique I use with my patients to help improve their skill for interpreting facial expressions and body language: Watch a few scenes of a movie you haven't seen before with the volume turned all the way down. Watch the facial expressions and nonverbal cues of the actors to see if you can capture the types of emotions they are projecting. Then rewatch the movie with dialog and see how closely your impressions match the story.

Even if you aren't good from the get-go, you should quickly improve with time. And once you're better at the movie game, you should be able to translate these sharpened skills for use in the real world. This is just one way of sharpening your interpretation of the world around you.

If you're feeling really brave, watch some home movies of yourself both with and without the sound. Pay close attention to your expressions, gestures, and other nonverbal communications. Is this the image you want to project to the world? Is it the image you thought you projected? Think about the things you do well to express yourself and the things that could use a few tweaks. It can be a very informative experience. You might also close your eyes and mentally rewind a social encounter to see if your impression of how you acted and were reacted to holds up.

as a drug-addicted prostitute. (She recounts her story in the excellent book *Snow Bodies: One Woman's Life on the Streets.*) We admire her resilience, her sense of humor, and, in this example, her stable sense of self in the face of adversity. In an interview with us, she described chatting with other moms at an event that took place a few years into her rehab.

"I was at a Tupperware party," she said, with a hint of amusement. "When you've lived 'the life' and you wind up sitting at a Tupperware party, there is part of your brain that goes, 'Oh, so they think what kind of diaper to use is a big deal when my life has been one of survival and fear and horror?'

"But in that moment I also realized that knowing the right diapers is kind of important if you don't want your children to have diaper rash. The women were teaching me how to live and have fun again, but the lessons learned from my past were valuable, too. They made me tougher and more resilient. Whatever my circumstances, it seems I have always retained the same basic humanity and sense of humor."

Throughout Hudson's life, her sense of Self-Awareness has remained surprisingly intact. Even the parts of her life that should be distorted by addiction and homelessness, she is able to recount with clarity. She always seems to know exactly who she is and was. This has served her well, and, as studies show, it's a display of true Winner's Brain thinking.

People who have a very stable sense of self, regardless of their present circumstances, tend to be long-term thinkers. When it comes to money, for instance, they are less likely to look to make a quick buck without considering whether or not there are better long-range options, a tendency economists and neuroscientists refer to as temporal discounting. One 2009 fMRI study by Hal Ersner-Hershfield and his Stanford University colleagues found that those who gave more consistent answers when asked to rate current personality traits, such as how courageous they are now versus how courageous they thought they might be at some future point in time, also showed the most consistent levels of cortical midline activity in the front-most region of the anterior cingulate. These individuals were also not as inclined toward temporal discounting as others in the study. Winners know that what is valuable today—whether it is a sense of humor or money—will probably also be valuable tomorrow, and perhaps even more so.

Minding Your Own Self

In her conversations with us, Hudson used the word "mindful" several times when describing how she views her past and how she approached creating her new life. Mindfulness connotes a present-centered, uncritical, and nonreactive way of thinking about yourself and your circumstances. It leads you to pay attention to your immediate emotions, thoughts, and body sensations without passing judgment or jumping into action. The goal of mindfulness is simply to be in the moment. From our conversation, it seems that such mindful acts may have helped Hudson loosen the grip that drug addiction had on her.

We also noticed Hudson naturally demonstrates an ability to name specific emotional states. Such a skill is often practiced in mindful endeavors such as yoga and meditation. Whereas many people have trouble putting a name to their emotional state of mind, she is very accurate and articulate when describing hers. When she talks about one of the dysfunctional relationships from her past, she vividly recalls feeling angry or sad or even amused at a particular moment about a particular event. Even while battling drugs, she was still very much in touch with her feelings and attitudes. It is not surprising to Hudson that there is evidence to show that this type of mindful thinking actually changes the way you use your brain.

In 2007, Matthew Lieberman and a team of University of California, Los Angeles investigators showed volunteers photographs of angry faces while monitoring activity in the amygdala, a region of the brain that is, among other things, associated with sounding the fear alarm in times of danger. Amygdala response was vigorous even when the researchers flashed the photos so quickly the volunteers couldn't tell what they were looking at. But when the volunteers were verbally told to match photos of angry faces with a word labeling the expression, something interesting happened. Their amygdalae calmed down while the regions of the brain associated with thinking about emotional experiences in words and controlling behavior lit up. By simply labeling what they were feeling with

Making Mindfulness Matter

Taking a regular yoga or meditation practice can be a great way to improve mindfulness skills, but there are simpler ways to practice, too. You can start by acknowledging how you feel at a particular point in time by stating it out loud. For example, just by saying, "I'm feeling angry right now" or "I'm feeling a lot of stress right now" or "This is joy" you gain greater control of how you react in a situation.

You can take it a step further by paying close attention to small details related to a particular emotional experience. When you are happy, notice the difference in your posture, your breath, and even the level of relaxation in your facial muscles versus how all of these things feel when you are depressed, angry, or flat. Practice creating emotional moments and consciously gathering information. You might look through a photo album or close your eyes to recall a past situation so you can stir up and reexamine emotions you felt in the past. Even shutting off your iPod, BlackBerry, and other technology for a few minutes a day to attend to your emotional state in the here and now helps develop the brain's mindfulness skills.

words, they were better able to control the parts of their brain responsible for overreaction and call upon greater neural resources to help them stay in Emotional Balance, moving them closer to ideal Winner's Brain behavior.

LOSING IT

One relatively new discovery is the importance of the superior frontal gyrus for the self. Using fMRI scans to measure brain activity, Ilan Goldberg and his Israeli colleagues at the Weizmann

Institute of Science found that the superior frontal gyrus was highly engaged during periods of introspective self-reflection compared to periods of a stimulus categorization control task. Subjects' ratings of their level of self-awareness were also much higher during these periods than during the control task. In contrast, when subjects were highly absorbed in a more demanding perceptual categorization task, the superior frontal gyrus regions appeared to largely shut down. This was accompanied by substantial reductions in ratings of self-awareness, almost as though the subjects literally lost their sense of self for a few moments. The researchers suggested that this temporary self-blindness may be part of the experience of "losing yourself" in the moment when engaged in a task.

Is Your Talent Meter Calibrated?

Having confidence in your strengths is clearly a good thing, but Winner's Brain Self-Awareness means getting a handle on your weaknesses, too. Science shows that those who remain in the dark about their shortcomings may unwittingly doom themselves to failure.

Cornell researchers David Dunning, Justin Kruger, and colleagues found that college students who scored in the bottom 25 percent on a course exam handed in their papers feeling like they had outperformed the majority of their peers. Some of the students were so blind to their ineptitude that even after scoring poorly on a test, they spent hours attempting to convince their professors that their answers were actually correct and the test was wrong!

Those who are blissfully unaware of their own deficiencies, it seems, don't know it, and they don't know that they don't know. Unfortunately for them, the parts of the brain that are involved with proficiency of a task are also often the same parts that handle proficiency awareness—so when you are bad at something, you may have no idea how bad you really are. This can be seen as the "double whammy of incompetence." If you've ever heard an obviously humor-impaired person attempt to tell a joke and then wonder aloud why no one got it, or watched an outtake segment of a talent-search reality show in which the jilted contestant is sure the judges have made a mistake ("But my singing was perfect! They don't know what they're talking about!"), you've witnessed the double whammy in all its glory.

When you're clueless as to why you've been unsuccessful at something, Dunning and colleagues recommend soliciting feedback. Ask for advice from people you trust, preferably someone who will hit you with honest yet constructive criticism. You might consider asking an expert or someone you consider a mentor to give you an honest critique of your talents and shortcomings. Having your faults laid bare may be tough to take, but it's a whole lot easier than repeatedly falling flat on your face. Another way to boost your brain's Talent Meter is by filling out a self-evaluation, having someone else do the same, and then comparing the two. This can be especially useful if you've been having trouble getting ahead at work and you aren't clear why. Finally, you can also try teaching someone else a skill you think you're good at. Often, if you have trouble explaining something to someone else, it means you yourself don't have a complete grasp of the information—unless of course your blind spot is thinking you're a good teacher when you're not.

Developing your sense of Self-Awareness not only helps you gauge how you are likely to react in a given situation, but it can also provide some insight into the people around you. Having a stable sense of self can therefore ground you in situations when many other circumstances are beyond your immediate control. In the next chapter, Motivation, you'll learn how a Winner's Brain is configured to get its owner going and keep him or her moving along to achieve his or her goals.

WIN FACTOR #2

Motivation

Cultivating the Drive to Win

MOTIVATION

Staying consistently motivated keeps you on a steady path toward success. Maintaining Motivation to plow through even the smallest or most mundane tasks is often just as important as being motivated by your overall goals.

Boost Your BrainPower: Think of Motivation as the fuel that keeps your Effort Accelerator going and the juice that helps keep your Goal Laser trained on the things that are important.

MARJORIE DESIMONE DIDN'T EXACTLY have all the advantages growing up. She lived on a dilapidated dairy farm in a poor rural Kentucky community. Her abusive father split when she was eight. Her mother was depressed and sick much of the time, eventually succumbing to cancer when DeSimone was just 14.

Despite the fact that no one in her family had ever attended college and she had little support from her school counselors—one told her to forget college and find work as a secretary—DeSimone refused to settle. She worked hard, made school a priority, and stayed focused on her goals, even after numerous false starts and failures. When her advisers wouldn't help her, she sat on her back staircase, slowly tapping out college applications on an old manual typewriter.

She went on to graduate with honors from Duke University and ultimately earned a master's degree in business from Harvard University. She's now a team leader with a top Fortune 500–friendly consulting firm, where she mentors today's future business leaders the way she wishes she had been mentored earlier in her own life.

Though her youth may sound like all stick and no carrot, DeSimone was still able to push herself and go on to achieve big things. Obstacles that would have stopped a less determined person cold challenged her Winner's Brain to continually strive. She could see the rewards even when they were a long way off and indeed, even when there were no guarantees she would ever be rewarded.

You could argue that DeSimone was simply lucky enough to have all the pieces come together as they did. But we maintain that luck is usually spun from the Winner's Brain characteristic of Motivation, and the mindset of being goal-oriented. In essence, Winners have the ability to make their own good fortune. We think Motivation has a lot to do with removing barriers (sometimes self-imposed) so you can clear the path and "begin to see the light at the end of the tunnel." Any potential you have remains untapped if you're unable to translate intention into action.

Map, Rev, Drive

There are some days when you wake up and you are in the zone. You're getting things done, you're focused, and you're clearing off items on your to-do list like a lumberjack chopping down trees. On days like these, it may feel like Motivation is something that hits you like a bolt of lightning; however, the science tells us otherwise. Considerable examination of motivation research suggests that Motivation flows through your brain in a three-phase process.

We call the first motivational phase *mapping* or *route planning* because this is when your brain maps out the trip to your final destination, i.e., your goals. Route planning is primarily the domain of the front half of the brain where structures such as the orbital-frontal cortex, amygdala, and striatum get busy evaluating and juggling information; they sift through all of the would-be objectives to see which are the most beneficial, weigh all of the potential risks, and calculate all of the possible outcomes until they lock in on the best goal under the circumstances.

Once these structures fix upon a goal, your brain flows into the *rev* phase of Motivation. Destination Goal has been entered into your neural GPS, and now you turn the key, adjust the mirrors, and give the engine a little gas. The neurotransmitter dopamine plays a key role in providing the "urge to do something" through a key neural pathway joining structures such as the ventral tegmental area in the midbrain and the nucleus accumbens in the ventral striatum. Motivated by the anticipation of reward associated with a successful outcome, these regions kick into gear with the limbic system, joining the efforts of the prefrontal cortex to move you from intention into action. We know from fMRI studies like the one done in 2007 at Duke University by Kari Eddington and her colleagues that these brain areas light up like Las Vegas when someone feels highly motivated and action oriented about a specific goal.

Drive is the third and final phase of Motivation. With map in hand and plenty of gas in the tank, the rubber hits the road. Mind you, this doesn't mean you cruise around aimlessly—drive is about moving in a very specific, goal-oriented direction. This momentum is sustained with help from the ventral striatum, the limbic system, and regions of the prefrontal cortex, particularly the orbital-frontal and adjacent medial prefrontal cortices.

When you form new goals, you begin the motivational cycle all over again. This can happen in a matter of seconds, over a long period of time, or anywhere in between. In the process of reaching a goal, you may bounce back and forth between route planning and rev a few times before there's enough gas in the engine to complete the journey, but you've got to go through the full map-rev-drive sequence in order to meet your objectives. This is true of any goal, whether it is learning a new language, completing a report at work, or simply heading out the door for a morning walk.

Whereas average brains often tend to stall out somewhere along the route, Winners are very good at cycling through the motivational loop again and again in order to achieve their goals on a consistent basis. From the most recent body of research available, a portrait of a motivated Winner is beginning to emerge. And whether Winners like the ones we feature in this chapter are this way by birth or through training or some combination thereof is sometimes impossible to say, but we do know that virtually everyone has it in them to be able to cultivate good motivational habits.

Tweezers and Trumpets

You may remember Trisha Meili's story from national headlines over the years. She's better known as the Central Park Jogger because of what happened to her one terrible night in April 1989. While out for a jog on the upper traverse of Central Park, she was brutally attacked, raped, and left for dead. Against incredible odds, she fought her way back from six weeks of coma and delirium, followed by several years of intense rehab. She's since gone on to achieve much with her life as a motivational speaker. For this, we consider her the epitome of a motivated Winner.

When she first arrived at Metropolitan Hospital, in a coma, with 75 percent blood loss, a fierce blow to the head and severe exposure, doctors worried that this young woman might not survive. The story seized the headlines, not only in New York but around the world as people contemplated the savagery of the attack. Meili survived, but it took months of intense therapy, hours a day, every day of the week, to learn how to walk again and retain basic, everyday skills like holding a fork and writing her name. Even after she left the hospital she trained at a private personal training gym for several years to regain balance, coordination, and stamina.

Meili told us about an incident that occurred near the beginning of her recovery while she was still a full-time patient at Gaylord Hospital in Wallingford, Connecticut. She was trying to regain the use of her hands. "In the process of regaining my manual dexterity I would perform an exercise with a wood board where I would use a pair of small tweezers to transfer nails into a series of holes," she recalls. "My mother could not believe my patience but I knew that at that moment it was what I had to do. I realized the only way I could improve my future was by working in the present."

It would have been easy for her to feel discouraged, frustrated, bored, or even very angry about having to work so hard to regain the basic skills most of us take for granted. But rehab, like most other long-term goals worth attaining, is the sum of countless small, anonymous victories. Meili focused on what she could do in the here and now. She knew if she wanted to use her hands again, worrying about the past or the future wasn't going to help. Staying in the present moment was where she needed to put her energy. "I looked at the reality that was mine, which was not good, but I worked as hard as I could to make it the best it could be," she says.

So many people find the Motivation to keep their Effort Accelerator humming along. Think of the scientist who does a thousand experiments to get to the one result that matters, the artist who spends months on a single painting, the mother who is teaching her child to write the alphabet one loop and line at a time. When we applaud the person who shows up to collect an award, we don't give much thought to specific tasks they had to do to get there. Even with raw talent and all the skills in the world, it probably meant dedicating an untold number of hours to the tedious, repetitive equivalents of Meili's tweezers-and-nails exercise.

In fact, the wherewithal to power through dull but necessary jobs you don't feel like doing seems to be something at which Winner's Brains excel. Consider the findings by Debra Gusnard and colleagues from Washington University School of Medicine. They scanned the brains of more than two dozen people who viewed a random combination of emotionally stimulating and thoroughly bland images and then asked them to fill out self-assessments related to their level of persistence for completing a series of mundane tasks. Differences in individual levels of persistence were related to differences in activity in the areas we associate with the drive phase of Motivation. Activity in the ventral striatum and orbital-frontal and nearby medial prefrontal cortices was higher when the tenaciously persistent Meilis of the group viewed the neutral pictures than when they were viewed by those who didn't score very well on follow-through. The researchers attributed this to persistent individuals' ability to stay focused even when they weren't all that excited by what they saw.

The motivational benefit of framing ordinary tasks in terms of the positive outcomes they produce can be traced to the effect it can have on activity in the amygdala. A recent study done at University College London by Benedetto De Martino and colleagues, for example, found amygdala activity depended on whether a given financial situation was framed in terms of what had been lost or in terms of what had been saved, and depended also on whether the subjects' response to this was to take a financial risk or go with a sure bet. This demonstrates the critical role that emotional evaluations can play in motivating behavior; finding the upside in the ordinary allows you to maximize your everyday life—and feel good about it. It also minimizes the lack of follow-through that often derails achievement.

It is also true that when something seems fresh and new it is much more stimulating than something old hat. So to the extent that you can find a way to feel inspired by the everyday tasks essential to reaching your goal, the more likely you are to complete the goal. This is thanks to the dopamine-rich ventral tegmental area in the midbrain, responsible for regulating Motivation and reward-processing. The burst of energy you feel when you try learning a new computer program or taste an unfamiliar cuisine is associated with the signals passed on by this brain region because of our preferences for novelty over the familiar.

Feeling the reward in everyday activities is important especially when goal attainment is a long way off, as with academic and career aspirations. Camille McDonald, the bright, dynamic president of brand development for Bath & Body Works, sums this concept up nicely: "Ninety-nine per-

Seize the Mundane

To grease the neural wheels of Motivation and stay on task, tune into the little voice inside your head that is constantly reminding you to tend to those seemingly insignificant matters like paying the bills, returning phone calls, and organizing your computer files. Start by making a checklist of those dull, daily tasks that have started to pile up and then think of a meaningful reason for getting them done: paying your bills on time helps you keep a close eye on your finances; returning phone calls is an efficient way to network and expose yourself to new opportunities; organizing your computer files saves time searching for the files you need and cuts down your workday.

cent of your life is spent getting there and so little time is spent holding the payoff in your hands. When you approach even the small, day-to-day issues with optimism and creativity, the journey is so much more enjoyable," she says.

McDonald's viewpoint has a good deal of scientific support. Psychologist Mihály Csíkszentmihályi proposed the idea of "flow" as a mental state in which a person is so fully immersed and so highly engaged in a well-practiced skill, she is able to break free and perform on autopilot. The positive energized experience that often accompanies such states can be highly rewarding in and of itself. Indeed, we share the view that motivational states such as these provide foundational blocks of creativity.

This was demonstrated in the brains of professional jazz musicians in an exciting 2008 study completed in Bethesda, Maryland, by Charles Limb and Allen Braun. On fMRI scans obtained during periods of improvisation versus rote performance, the musical flow experienced by these talented artists was associated with a disengagement of regions of

Find the Pearl

One method of finding new ways of looking at things is through another person's eyes. If you're an expert at something, show your project to a non-expert and get their impression. Ask a child what they see—talk about a fresh set of eyes! You can also try giving a redundant task or situation a new backdrop. If you always eat lunch at your desk, try taking it in the park or sit next to the beautiful painting in the lobby. Or try mixing up the details. Have you ever had breakfast for dinner? You should. Pancakes taste different at six p.m. than at six a.m. Even small tweaks to your routines can breathe new life into them.

the dorsal lateral prefrontal cortex associated with cognitive control and enhanced recruitment of sensorimotor regions and areas of the medial prefrontal cortex. Such free-flowing improvisation is something less skilled and talented musicians don't seem to be able to do. The authors of the study suggest that the regions the musicians were able to shut down during improvisation are closely related to policing thoughts in order to control both thoughts and behavior. Once they were able to set their brains free, creativity soared.

Flow state can take many forms, as with a modern dancer who moves with the music, a mathematician lost in solving an equation, an executive like McDonald flawlessly executing a marketing campaign, or when you come up with clever solutions to common problems at work.

"If you're not an artist, a composer, or a musician, can you still be creative? I can't do any of those things but at some point I realized I am extremely creative," McDonald says. "In my line of work I tell people a story that makes them happy and give them the product that replicates

Go with the Flow

If you have trouble achieving flow state, try coming at a problem or a task from the opposite direction: Focus on each of the steps that lead to your goal rather than the outcome. For example, if your goal is to write a book, don't just concentrate on seeing your book in the bookstore. Write down a list of all the tasks that go into writing a book. You might talk to a friend who has written a book to better understand the process. Next, you might outline the book. Then you might look at similar books. And so on. Start by completing one task—call that author friend to get her input. Paradoxically, the joy you find in completing one thing that moves you forward may be just the thing that pushes you into a higher state of mind. It allows your brain to let go and roam free—to flow.

that story and at the same time, I'm also looking at things like whether or not the financials make sense. The process of pulling that all together is like conducting a symphony."

Rewards Inside and Out

As we'll talk about more in Win Factor #6, Resilience, the belief that your efforts are meaningful and have influence over the outcome is called an *internal locus of control*. It's classic Winner's Brain thinking, and from a motivational standpoint, it's like having a full tank of premium fuel for the map-rev-drive sequence.

People with an internal point of view tend to value what psychologists refer to as *intrinsic* rewards like personal satisfaction, better health, or happier relationships, as opposed to *external* rewards such as money and material things. They often choose to delay gratification for a bigger payoff rather than the here-and-now quick fix. As a result, they seem better equipped to aim for large, productive, long-term goals than their external counterparts.

When the former LPGA golf great talked to us about what motivates her, she never once mentioned money, even though she has obviously earned a fortune thanks to her considerable talents. "I choose my opportunities based on what I can learn from them," she explains. "I enjoy the process of learning and when I find something I am interested in I put my brain and my time into it."

Harvard professor of business administration Teresa M. Amabile has made a career studying the effects of intrinsic versus extrinsic reward on creativity and productivity. Her numerous studies have found, somewhat paradoxically, that this view is correct: Focusing on the cash, trophies, and other types of material gain is often a performance killer. Intrinsic interest in a task—the sense that something is worth doing for its own sake—typically diminishes when someone is rewarded for doing it and, if the reward becomes the primary reason for doing something, the activity becomes less enjoyable. In one study, for instance, Amabile found that children who "contracted for a reward" before the start of an art project were consistently judged by their teachers as turning in the least creative work.

It seems that productivity and external reward are inversely proportional after a certain threshold. To begin with, extrinsic rewards tend to encourage people to focus narrowly on a task, to do it as quickly as possible, and to take few risks. They focus on getting the prize and less on the creative process of reaching the goal. Second, they often begin to feel as if they are being controlled by the reward, so they tend to be less invested and less performance-oriented than if they were doing it for the sense of accomplishment or even a compliment from the boss. The less self-determined they feel, the more their creative juices dry up. And lastly, focus on extrinsic rewards can erode intrinsic interest. People who see themselves as working for money, approval, or competitive success find their tasks less pleasurable, and therefore have more trouble getting them done.

So, though it may seem like a good idea to dangle a larger bonus in front of an employee to get her to put her nose closer to the grindstone or a larger allowance in front of a teenager to make A's, the Harvard research calls into question the widespread belief that this will be effective. Without an innate sense of Motivation for the more abstract reasons like prestige, self-satisfaction, and a sense of accomplishment, you will tend to go about completing your tasks in a less creative and productive manner. The key is to find the reward somewhere in the journey.

However, that said, there *are* times when extrinsic rewards can be useful. It all comes down to how the reward is perceived. If you view yourself as working for the primary purpose of "getting something," the activity ceases to be worth doing for its own sake. But when Motivation is in short supply, extrinsic rewards can be useful in getting you over the hump. No one knows this better than the University of Pennsylvania's Kevin Volpp, who has made a career of exploring the idea of offering rewards to people trying to improve their health habits.

One of Volpp's recent studies, published in February 2009, looked at offering financial incentives in exchange for kicking the tobacco habit. Employees of a large national company received $100 if they participated in a smoking-cessation program and $250 if they quit smoking any time in the first six months. If they didn't light up again for another six months, they received an additional $400. Those who were randomly assigned to receive the cash incentive tripled the typical long-term quit rate when Volpp's team checked up on them nine to 12 months after enrollment. And when they checked in on them six months after they stopped getting the cash, they found that the long-term quit rates were still 2.6 times higher compared to people who tried to go smoke free without any monetary enticement.

But why was this? Wouldn't the Harvard research suggest the opposite result? In this case there seems to be another factor at play. There are

Try Stepping-Stone Goals

The lesson Volpp's work teaches us is that, when you're having trouble staying motivated toward a particular, long-term goal, setting a series of short-term material goals can help you stay focused. And while the act of getting a college education is a noble aspiration in and of itself, there's nothing wrong with promising yourself a tropical vacation for making A's this semester. Material rewards can be effective motivational stepping stones so long as you keep them in perspective and your long-term goals truly have personal meaning.

times you might need a little push, such as some cash or merchandise, to get yourself moving, but in the long run it is unlikely this will continue to motivate you. You may quit smoking for the $100, but unless you like the benefits of coughing less, clear lungs, a lower risk of cancer, and the money savings you enjoy as a result, it is unlikely you will stay smoke-free for very long.

"One of the problems with smoking is that it's always more difficult to quit than not quit. So, in the present, it's easier to remain a smoker despite the long-term health risks and this contributes to procrastination," Volpp notes. "The incentive program helped people overcome some of their initial inertia and provided tangible feedback in the short term which proved to be sufficiently motivating." Volpp stresses that because tobacco is exceptionally addictive, it is difficult to initiate and maintain the resolve to quit. Cash rewards appear to provide the motivational jump start needed to get past the initial challenges.

When you dig deeper, you see that the cash payout alone cannot be the only impetus for quitting. A smoker would save about $1,500 a year by kicking the habit on their own, double the maximum they could earn by participating in the study. Volpp suspects that people who volunteer for the program have greater-than-average intrinsic Motivation to begin with and they perceive value in simply participating. For them, this makes winning money more motivating than saving money. Volpp also speculates that once people got past the initial pain of quitting, additional intrinsic rewards like breathing easier, less coughing, and better-smelling clothes kicked in.

The Flip Side of Motivation

We kept putting off writing this chapter on Motivation. Apparently we're not alone. According to University of Calgary procrastination expert Piers Steel, about 95 percent of academics are procrastinators and about 50 percent chronically so. Procrastination costs time, productivity, stress, and yes, money too; Steel cites a survey by the Gail Kasper Consulting Group in Philadelphia which found that the 40 percent of Americans who wait until the last minute to file their taxes cost themselves an average of $400.

Why do we have a tendency to postpone a task when it's obviously better to simply get it done? In January 2009, Sean McCrea and a team of psychologists set out to find the answer through students from the University of Konstanz in Germany. They began by handing out questionnaires to the students and then asked them to respond by email within three weeks. The questions all related to the mundane task of opening a bank account, but some students were asked about abstract concepts like what kind of person has a bank account while others were asked about the nuts and bolts of opening an account such as filling out forms and making an initial deposit. The idea was to see if giving the first group some "psychological distance" from the task made a difference in how quickly they responded.

It did. Even though all of the students knew they would be paid for sending the questionnaire back, the ones given the more abstract questions were much more likely to procrastinate—in some cases the researchers are still waiting for a reply. Those who were focused on the more tangible aspects of the task sent their responses much sooner, suggesting that they sat down and got it done without delay. So, if you want to avoid procrastinating, concentrate on concrete rather than intangible aspects of your task. It's hard to put something into action if you don't have a grasp on the details.

COLOR ME MOTIVATED

Red flashing lights mean danger. Errors are highlighted in red. And we all know too well what red numbers on a balance sheet mean. A team of scientists led by the University of Rochester's Andrew Elliot says that the idea that red means bad is so ingrained in most of us that even getting a glimpse of scarlet before taking a test or performing an important task can profoundly affect achievement.

In their 2007 study, the researchers briefly flashed the color red in front of people right before they took a series of important achievement tests, like IQ or a major exam, and found that even the subtlest exposure to the hue led to substantially poorer performance. The electroencephalography (EEG) study done as part of the investigation mapped greater relative right frontal cortex activation when a subject was exposed to red than with other colors. This type of brain activity has been linked to avoidance Motivation; in other words, the Motivation to avoid failure rather than to achieve success—not exactly the most productive attitude when you're trying to ace a test.

The moral of the story? When you have something important to accomplish, avoid seeing red at all costs.

A Task Master

If you find yourself procrastinating on a task, try thinking about it in very specific, concrete terms to make it feel like it must be completed sooner. As we mentioned in "Go with the Flow," break the project up into small, manageable parts, then try completing just one chunk of it. Whether you organize your home one drawer at a time, finish up a big report for work one paragraph at a time, or begin the repair of a relationship with one email, you get the ball rolling and reduce the size of the task so it immediately feels more manageable. Start with something small; a series of small steps adds up to a whole staircase.

Trisha Meili showed you that it's possible to stay motivated by focusing on what you can do in the here and now. Winners know luck has nothing to do with success; you make your own "luck" by valuing both the process and the outcome of the tasks you face. This is critical for maintaining your drive for even small, dull tasks that contribute to your larger goals. Though it may not have been obvious before you read this chapter, you now know Motivation is actually the key to creativity because it helps you stay focused as needed. In fact, the neural architecture underlying such changes in Focus, which you'll learn about in the next chapter, fits hand in glove with the brain circuits for Motivation.

WIN FACTOR #3

Focus

Locking on
to What's Important

FOCUS

In this chapter, you'll learn how to maintain the flexibility to use the type of Focus you need for each particular situation. Winners have a wonderful ability to focus on the most important details. And by incorporating details into your broad Focus, your brain will become more innovative, flexible, and creative.

Boost Your BrainPower: Your Goal Laser and Effort Accelerator rely on Focus to stay locked on your goals and to create the synergy needed to keep moving forward. Strong Focus skills also mean you are watching the screen when the right blip appears on your Opportunity Radar screen.

A S THE LAST U.S. PERFORMER in the vault finals of the 1996 Olympics in Atlanta, 17-year-old Kerri Strug was the U.S. women's gymnastics team's final hope of capturing their first-ever Olympic gold medal in the all-around competition.

Her first attempt ended in disaster: Strug landed unevenly, her legs buckled, and she fell backwards, severely spraining her left ankle and tearing two ligaments in the process.

Strug was in trouble and obviously in a great deal of pain. But unless she aced the second vault, her dreams, as well as the team's collective hopes, would vanish. The world watched and waited to see what she would do.

Strug opted to do the final vault. The television cameras recorded the wince of pain as she hopped on one leg to the start position. A tight close-up on her face revealed deep concentration as she paused to gather herself before sprinting towards the vault. The crowd went silent as her hands hit the top of the horse.

Her vault was virtually flawless, and she nailed the landing, raising her hands high in the air to salute the judges before lifting her injured leg off the mat. As she went to her knees in pain, the crowd roared. The U.S. Women's Gymnastics Team now owned a gold medal. Kerri Strug's face relaxed just a little.

What Is Focus?

In one of the most memorable moments in Olympic history, Strug provides a beautiful example of the Winner's Brain trait we call Focus. William James, 19th-century Harvard psychologist and philosopher, alluded to a definition of Focus by saying, "It is the taking possession of the mind, in clear and vivid form, of one out of what seem several simultaneous possible objects or trains of thought. . . . Focalization, concentration, of consciousness are of its essence. It implies withdrawal from some things in order to deal effectively with others. . . ." Focus involves attention and concentration. Thus, a simpler way to define it is in terms of the mental energy required to gather significant details and tune out unnecessary distractions.

"I've always been focused," says Strug, now 29 and a special adviser in children's affairs to the Department of Justice. "Even as a child I was never a procrastinator." Hearing a statement like that from someone as obviously focused as Strug tends to confirm most people's belief that Focus is something you either have or you don't. But that's not true. Practice and training can dramatically improve your powers of concentration. Innate though her Focus may have been, years of gymnastics training helped Strug hone those gifts to perfection.

Winner's Brains are flexible; they have a tremendous ability to calibrate the level of Focus across a broad range of circumstances. By using a variety of strategies, they can fine-tune the neural machinery of Focus to provide a distinct advantage. And amazingly, nurturing these powers of attention and concentration can actually change the physical makeup of the brain itself, often directly translating into improved Focus.

Blips, Bleeps, and Blinks

Strug's vault, which at the time was viewed by millions of people all over the world, is now a classic YouTube moment. Watching the video, even through the lens of time, you still feel the chills of anticipation as Strug charges down the runway. Will she nail the landing? Will the United States get the gold?

"I get questions all the time about what I was thinking in those seconds before I did my second vault," Strug says. "People want to know how I dealt with the pain and how I was still able to perform."

Her explanation is simple: "There's not much time between vaults so I thought to myself, 'You fell and jarred your ankle but it doesn't matter what's wrong because you're going to do it anyway.' Then, I was so well trained I just focused on the task at hand. I didn't hear the crowd or think about my ankle or what was riding on my success or failure, I just concentrated on my performance. I said to myself, 'OK, here we go!' And that was it. For that moment, I was on autopilot."

Top athletes aren't the only ones who experience situations where it all comes down to one instance. Every one of us has taken a test, delivered a presentation, or given a performance that we perceived to be make-or-break. Different Winner's Brain traits come into play here, but it's the ability to really concentrate and maintain a *narrow focus* that enables us to triumph.

If you've ever watched thoroughbred racing, you may have noticed some of the horses wearing a piece of head gear called blinkers, which look like two leather drink coasters placed on the outermost edges of their eyes for the humane purpose of restricting peripheral vision. Well, a state of narrow focus is the mind's version of blinkers. It's the type of focus you need when you're doing a task that requires your absolute attention. In recounting the shining moment of her gymnastics career, Strug doesn't remember external factors like the sound of the spectators or her throbbing ankle. She tuned into what she needed to do.

For most of us, narrow focus is a skill reserved for practical, routine situations like preparing taxes or sewing on a button, tasks that require the ability to block out all unnecessary, unwanted information to concentrate on one thing. Clearly, mind-wandering and attentional missteps in these sorts of situations cause us to make mistakes: Let your mind drift off while threading a needle and you get a sharp reminder of why it's important to pay attention.

Buttons and taxes are the least of it. The average person contends with an astonishing number of distractions. One survey found the average office worker switches tasks every three minutes and once interrupted takes nearly half an hour to go back to the original task. Between email, instant messaging, cell phones, Twitter, BlackBerries, iPhones, TV, and digital signage, attention is a casualty of the high-tech age we live in. So rampant are distractions, they've spawned a new field called interruption science. They've also helped coin the word "single-tasking" to describe the luxury of being able to give your undivided attention to one thing at a time.

One recent investigation into a type of distraction called a brain blip, or in more technical terms, an *attentional lapse,* was carried out by a team of researchers led by Daniel Weissman, a cognitive neuroscientist at the University of Michigan. Weissman and his colleagues wanted to know what happens at the neural level during a brain blip, so they asked a group of volunteers to look out for two symbols among a series of symbols that flashed randomly across a screen and then push a button each time one of the symbols popped up. As the participants went about searching for symbols and pressing buttons, the Weissman team was busy scanning their brains and measuring the localized changes in blood oxygen levels that follow changes in brain activity. Subjects were given all the time they needed to give the correct response to each visual display.

The researchers noted that reaction time varied substantially both between subjects and among the same subjects from one test to the next. Faster reaction times meant the person was locked and loaded on the task at hand—paying attention—whereas slower reaction times meant that the person was briefly distracted.

As the researchers monitored the different brain images and the different areas of the brain that lit up, they found some interesting differences in brain activity depending on reaction time. Slower reaction times were associated with reduced activity in the anterior cingulate and prefrontal cortices, structures of the brain thought to help in controlling attentional focus. Importantly, this reduction of activity in these regions occurred before the visual pattern popped up, which is consistent with the possibility that the person experienced an attentional lapse moments before the trial took place. There was also reduced activation in the visual-processing areas at the rear of the brain, as if those areas had not been properly notified by the distracted regions of the frontal lobe that it was time to spring into action.

Another type of Focus-related processing error people often make was reported in 1992 by Jane Raymond, now at Bangor University in Wales, and her colleagues while then at the University of Calgary. Researching a completely different topic, she and her team devised a study involving a rapid-fire stream of individual letters flickering onto a screen and asking volunteers to spot each of two pre-specified targets. When she and her team examined the results, they noticed that if a second target appeared within a half a second or so after the first target, people failed to see it. Raymond instantly realized she had hit upon something important. She dubbed this temporary "mind blindness," caused by the fact that we aren't good at taking in two things at once, an *attentional blink.*

Says Raymond, "The name 'attentional blink' came to me because we were also doing some eye movement studies during visual perception and I noticed that people habitually blink just when a trial ends. It seemed to me that when an attentional episode is over, the attentional system does just what the eyes do—blink!" In subsequent investigations, researchers have discovered that the attentional blink also happens for images of faces, objects, and TV ads laced with grabby images (bad news for advertisers using quick-cut imagery to get their products noticed).

There's more. University of Delaware researcher Steven Most has identified a phenomenon he calls *attentional rubbernecking,* which is similar to what you experience when you're driving along on a highway and can't take your eyes off an accident; your focus is on the wreck instead of the road and then—wham! You've crashed too. Then there's *inattentional blindness,* a phrase coined by psychologists Arien Mack and Irvin Rock, which refers to the inability to see something if you're not paying attention, even if it's right in front of you. This time you crash the car because, while busy watching for oncoming traffic, you fail to notice the deer standing smack in the middle of the road.

All these blips, bleeps, and blinks of Focus are manifestations of the same problem: Despite having more than 100 billion neurons at our disposal acting as super high-speed neural processors, our attentional resources can only be stretched so thin. When we dedicate those resources to processing one thing in the environment, we often don't have the resources to allocate to another. Our mind must stop and catch its breath for a moment, so to speak, before it's able to move on and process the next piece of information.

Beating Distractions

The Weissman study reveals a few clues about how we might be able to reduce attentional load in everyday, practical situations. His subjects' error rates were about the same regardless of whether they performed quickly or slowly. When they were slow to respond, the researchers realized subjects compensated for the delay in brain activity before the task began, with greater brain activity once the person engaged and was actively trying to solve the problem. In other words, the pre-test brain blip was offset by an extra dose of attention when the person was actually engaged in searching for the symbol on the screen. Yes, a momentary distraction cost more time—but this extra time helped the subjects avoid making mistakes.

Get your brain back on task after it's been distracted with this simple, yet effective Winner's Brain strategy we call *focus reinvestment.* If you find yourself in the middle of something that requires a lot of Focus, stop

Five Easy Steps to Reinvest Your Focus

1. Admit to yourself you're off task.

2. Remind yourself of the original task and why it's important.

3. If possible, eliminate the factors that derailed your attention; turn off cell phone, close email, grab a sandwich, finish a conversation.

4. Choose a starting point, cue yourself with a word like "go" and get back on task, noticing the rich details of what you are doing. If you're reading something you're trying to stay focused on, put a checkmark at the bottom of every page or every so often, jot a word in the margin.

5. Pay attention to the small details you may not ordinarily notice to give you a new perspective on the task at hand.

and consciously reorient yourself to critical details. Pay attention to minutiae like sounds, textures, and colors you might not ordinarily notice. For example, right before you are about to give a speech, you might deliberately notice the fabric of the chair you're sitting in or the tone of the previous speaker's voice. You'll find that this helps you gather your Focus and turn down the volume on fear, nervousness, or any other competing brain buzz.

Some winners, like African-born Tommy Frank, come by this focus reinvestment technique naturally. As a New York City window washer for more than twenty years working often dozens of stories up from the ground, Frank certainly has much to lose from poor focus. "I can never allow myself to think about other things in the middle of a job," he says.

"I'm focused on my own safety, checking the belt and ropes and so forth each time I clip in or out; I make sure I keep track of all my tools so I don't accidentally drop any on a pedestrian below; I concentrate on the type of window I'm cleaning, all of the hinges and the screws so I don't open it the wrong way or allow the glass to fall out."

The concept of focus reinvestment to reduce mind wandering illustrates another important finding of the Weissman study. Not only were the research subjects able to boost brain activity after a pre-test distraction, they were also usually able to add an extra burst of brain activity after a slower reaction time so they were able to maintain Focus and respond more quickly in subsequent trials. It was as if the subjects literally "learned their lesson" following an attentional lapse and actually changed the way their brains worked. They weren't able to make this happen every time, but when they did, their response times were even faster without compromising accuracy. This suggests that you can truly reorient after a brain lapse and get back on track.

Another Winner's Brain strategy for dealing with distractions is minimizing or avoiding them in the first place. In one fascinating study, Heleen Slagter and her University of Wisconsin–Madison colleagues gave a group of 17 volunteers a classic attentional blink test and then had them study a yoga/meditation technique that emphasized reducing distraction and enhancing awareness. After three months of study, the subjects then took the test again. Lo and behold, the volunteers' abilities to avoid an attentional blink and see the second symbol improved significantly—and further, their ability to see the first symbol didn't suffer.

This suggested to the researchers that meditation training makes the brain more efficient at distributing its neural resources. Thus, the volunteers seemed able to devote fewer of those resources to the first task, leaving enough left over to attend to another target that followed shortly after. Indeed, a reduced amount of brain activity associated with seeing the

Play to Win

Video games may seem the complete antithesis of meditation, but in fact they have a positive impact on attentional focus. Research conducted at the University of Rochester by Shawn Green and Daphne Bavelier revealed vast improvements in attention control after just ten hours of video game play. (Parents of a Grand Theft Auto–obsessed teenager probably didn't need a study to convince them of this!) But as we offer up a few hours on the Wii as a novel way to enrich your Focus abilities, a cautionary note: There's a fine line here between Winner's Brain strategy and too much of a good thing.

first symbol strongly predicted the ability to accurately detect the second one. The subjects weren't meditating at the time they were being tested, which implies that their mindfulness training had paid off with lasting and significant benefits to their powers of attentional control.

The subjects' meditation practice in the Slagter study was quite rigorous—up to 12 hours a day—but numerous other studies show that even a little can go a long way, including a 2007 investigation at the University of Pennsylvania by Amishi Jha and colleagues, which found that practicing even small doses of daily meditation can improve Focus. Another study published later that same year by Chinese researcher Yi-Yuan Tang and her colleagues showed positive effects on attentional control in just five days of meditation practices lasting a mere 20 minutes per day. In both of these studies, the subjects were casual students of meditation. Of course, it stands to reason that the more time and effort you put in, the more benefits you'll reap. (Note: We cover meditation in depth in both the Brain Care and Adaptability chapters.)

Practice, Practice, Practice

As you may already suspect, on the opposite end of the spectrum from using a narrow focus is using a *wide focus,* the type of Focus we use to survey, manage, and integrate multiple factors from our external surroundings or internal thoughts. Rather than lavish all your attentional resources on one small detail, wider focus calls for spreading them across a larger canvas. This is the type of Focus the brain of a symphony conductor flips to when he's conducting a piece of music and he must read the music score, cue each section, and listen to the tone of the overall orchestra while integrating the sound of each individual instrument.

It's also the type of Focus Geoff Billingsley needed as an air force major. When asked to recount his most memorable experience as a pilot, Billingsley, who trained fighter jet and B-2 bomber pilots for more than eight years, calmly relates a story that perfectly illustrates how a Winner's Brain uses wide focus:

> I was up with a student in a T-37 trainer jet. We had climbed to 20,000 feet and purposely put the aircraft into a tailspin so we could practice getting out of it. This was one of those standard things I drilled with student pilots so they were not encountering it for the first time in the heat of battle.
>
> The plane had stalled and we were completely out of air speed. As the plane spiraled, I was conscious of the ground rushing towards us, making a mental note that it was getting closer at the rate of 3,000 feet per minute. I waited a few turns to see if my student would begin to initiate recovery procedures and when he didn't I calmly turned to him and said, "Idle. Neutral. Aft. Spinning right-needle right. Full left rudder. One full turn Stick, abruptly full forward and hold, then Stick neutral and recover from dive."
>
> That's the sequence for spin recovery procedure, and it's one of those things a pilot needs to know verbatim. In the air force, it's what

we call a bold-faced command and any experienced pilot can recite it in his sleep. My student didn't have the huge bank of flight experience a seasoned pilot has to draw on, but he'd done enough training to be able to recite and perform the spin recovery procedure checklist by heart.

He got through the first three steps OK: Push the stick abruptly forward and hold until the nose drops down and the plane is perpendicular to the ground. The jet is set up on its nose and in a position where you can grab enough air to recover from the spin.

That's when he froze.

As we started to pitch past vertical, his hands gripped the stick and his elbows locked full force. It's essential to complete the recovery sequence quickly so the plane doesn't stay perpendicular to the ground for too long; otherwise it goes into an inverted spin where it's still rotating around and around, but now it's upside down. All things considered, not an ideal situation.

"Release the stick," I said firmly.

Nothing.

"Okay. I have the aircraft," I told him, reaching over to take the controls.

Nothing. Still no reaction.

At this point, time started to slow down and I remember thinking "Does he hear me? Am I saying something that just doesn't translate? Or is he thinking he can do this and he simply doesn't want to give me control of the aircraft?" In the same instant, I considered all my options. Maybe I could say the sequence in a different way? Try different words? Or, I could try the strong-arm approach and wrestle the controls from him. But would that make him think there was something wrong with the plane and if so, how would he react? In the end, I karate chopped him across the elbows. That was enough to break his spell—and his grip. I took control of the jet and we recovered from the dive.

Don't you immediately suspect a Winner's Brain at work here? Billingsley's ability to stay level-headed and keep a wide focus in a life-or-death pressure situation is extraordinary. He was able to pull out the correct resolution by sifting through all of the potential distracters including the plane and its swiftly changing position and altitude, the student pilot's demeanor, his actions, and several potential options. And he did this all in a slice of time no more than a few seconds long.

Clearly this shows distraction isn't just a prospective problem during narrow focus; it has the potential to muck up your ability to skillfully use a wide focus too. It would have been easy for Billingsley to get caught up in the irrelevant details. He might have been distracted by the sensation of the plane spinning around or a rush of air through the cockpit cabin or the buzzing of the instruments on the control panel. None of these factors would have helped him troubleshoot his way to safety, especially in the few precious seconds he had to decide upon the best course of action.

Like Kerri Strug's use of narrow focus to complete her vault, Billingsley could not have pulled off his feat of cool-headed wide focus without all the technical aspects of spin recovery procedure tattooed into his memory. The cockpit of a military jet is crammed with expansive control panels featuring over 150 dials, switches, levers, and buttons. Pilots spend two to three years in training, on average, during which they log hundreds of hours committing every feature and control of the aircraft to memory. They endlessly drill every likely—and unlikely—scenario they might encounter so by the time training is complete, they've learned to fly with their brains literally switched to autopilot.

Control over widening and narrowing focus is much greater when a task is practiced to the point of being automatic because it's easier to free up neural resources when you don't waste attentional energy thinking through each of the meticulous steps involved. Well-automated tasks and thought processes reduce the load on attention and Focus by habitually ensuring that the brain relies on implicit memory—implicit in the sense

Cruise Control to New Heights

The more tasks you can automate and the more information you can shift to implicit memory, the lighter the load on the attention systems and the more control you gain over your powers of Focus and concentration. And in fact, this leads us to an essential Winner's Brain strategy for sharpening your Focus skills: Practice, practice, practice—until you can perform on autopilot.

that we don't have to consciously retrace the steps of our previous experience with a task to complete it.

Every time you tie your shoes you don't say to yourself, "Now take one lace in each hand, make an X, draw the top lace through the bottom of the X, pull the two laces tight, make a loop out of each lace so you create bunny ears . . ." and so on (though you probably did something like this when you were first learning how to do it). Now, you simply tie your shoes without any conscious thought, often while doing something else like talking on the phone or watching television. Repetition to the point of autopilot is like clearing off an extra shelf in your brain: You pack up recurring pieces of information and store them in implicit memory, which frees up room for focusing on those important aspects that still require conscious thought and control.

Pilots use many techniques for consigning very complex chunks of information into implicit memory. Besides all the flight time they log, both in a simulator and in an actual plane, they memorize hundreds of checklists, standard sequences, and mnemonic devices. And Kerri Strug says if she did ten vaults in practice and fell on the tenth one she would never just walk away and let herself end on a bad routine—so the Olympic drama was no different, except this time the whole world was watching. In other words, she rehearsed her gymnastic skills *and* her emotional responses in all different types of situations.

Of course it's obvious that practice leads to skill improvement, but a large part of that improvement boils down to the fact that attention is a finite resource; if your brain is busy fumbling around trying to remember how to do something, too many resources get dedicated to the rote aspects of the job. You experience this phenomenon in the early stages of studying a new language when it takes a long time to form a sentence because you're caught up trying to keep the rules of grammar straight, or when first learning how to play chess and you're so overwhelmed with trying to remember the names of the pieces and how they're allowed to move, you can't stay focused on the game.

Break It Down

By the way, it's probably not the best idea to jump in and try your equivalent of a Yurchenko 1½ twist vault or attempt a tailspin recovery on your first day in the cockpit. When you're learning something that involves a lot of complexity or that requires you to focus, try *scaffolding* it, a technique where you practice the individual parts of a skill in a stepwise fashion before putting them all together as a whole.

Pilots-in-training, for example, spend a lot of their time "chair flying" before they actually attempt a flight skill in an actual aircraft. In chair flying, they set up a swivel chair, place a toilet plunger on the floor between their knees, don their helmet and oxygen mask, and then try to mimic every aspect of a flight in their mind. Billingsley says that no detail was too small to be left out during chair flight, and he would even take it down to where he would place his bag when he first arrived at the aircraft. "I might start out in the morning and spend the whole day in chair flight, just thinking and practicing. I'd chair fly a sequence repeatedly,

Visualization Made Simple

Make it vivid: Use all of your senses to make the experience real.

Choose a perspective: When you visualize, are you looking through your own eyes or are you watching yourself on a stage? Some research suggests using the audience perspective is most beneficial.

Visualize in real time: That's the speed you'll use in reality.

Maximize control: You control everything that happens in visualization—successes, comebacks, other people's reactions, etc. Use that control to take yourself where reality may or may not go.

and then sure enough when I sat in the simulator or the jet, that training kicked in as soon as I hit step one," he says.

Many sports and vocations have their own version of chair flying to help visualize their skills. Golfers close their eyes to picture a swing and top salespeople spend a lot of time refining their pitch to the customer. As you'd expect, this practice and visualization cause the areas of the brain responsible for simulating a task to light up—but the parts of the brain responsible for actually performing a task light up as well, suggesting that they help you perform better in real time. So it appears that thinking can be almost as good as doing.

Use Your Zoom

A Winner's Brain is also especially adept at toggling effortlessly back and forth between narrow and wide focus at the appropriate times. In 1986, two researchers at the University of Illinois at Urbana-Champaign,

The ABCs of Prioritizing

There are many systems for helping to cultivate the Winner's Brain strategy of setting priorities. This method, used by people who swear by the Franklin Planner organizational system, is as easy as ABC.

* Start by writing a list of everything you need to accomplish; list every task you can think of as it comes to mind without worrying about the particular order.

* Next assign each task an A, B, or C ranking where A is assigned to high-priority tasks that need to be completed within a day, B to tasks that need to be completed within a week, and C to tasks that need to be completed within a month.

* Now subdivide each category by ranking them in numerical order with your number one task designated A1, your next priority A2, and so on.

* Revisit the list daily and reassess priorities as needed. Make a fresh list at the start of each week.

Charles Eriksen and James St. James, first likened this ability to a camera's zoom lens where you turn the dials and adjust a few settings to zoom in on a narrow part of the picture or zoom out to capture the whole scene. Their studies were among the first to describe this as a dynamic process.

Recent fMRI studies, such as that led by Joseph Orr at the University of Michigan, show how specialized areas of the anterior cingulate cortex (ACC), an oblong structure located in the central region of the frontal lobe, light up when you need to adjust your Focus. The ACC is sensitive to incoming information that might conflict with an ongoing task or sequence of thoughts. It plays a critical role in detecting potential distractions and in signaling other parts of the brain, mainly in the outer, lateral regions of the frontal and parietal lobes, to boost attention to what is most relevant for what we want to do.

Winners seem to be able to train their brain to have ACCs that work with this frontal-parietal attention network to ensure the right type of Focus at the right time and avoid a potential "can't see the forest for the trees" or "can't see the trees for the forest" type of conundrum. If Billingsley had begun trying to resolve the tailspin by directing his attention to a single "tree," like say, the position of the plane, he would have missed the rest of the "forest," the altitude, speed, the student, all of the potential solutions. If his Focus had continued to evaluate the multiple factors of the situation, the solution of karate chopping the student's elbows would have remained a tree hidden in the forest. Meditation may be a helpful way to practice adjusting your zoom lens since it specifically trains the brain to alter its level of Focus; research indicates that meditation can thicken the regions associated with attentional control and thus improves the ability to concentrate.

Getting Your Priorities Straight

Practice, scaffolding, and the zoom lens all lead to the point of why you pay attention in the first place, and that's for the purpose of setting priorities. When you prioritize, you use what limited attentional resources you have at your disposal to juggle information in the most effective, efficient manner possible. Winners continuously bring a situational factor to the top of the list, examine it, eliminate it if necessary, and then move the next item to the top of the list. Even in a high-stress situation, a winner can do this spontaneously and instantaneously. When Billingsley, for example, steadily reevaluated his predicament, he demonstrated a high level of prioritization expertise.

Here again, meditation can help. The 2007 study by Jha and colleagues at the University of Pennsylvania found 30 minutes of meditation helped subjects raise their ability to prioritize and manage tasks and goals after just one month. After eight weeks those both experienced and novice in the art and practice of mindfulness performed faster and more accurately on a series of computer skills similar to those any computer user would encounter. The results suggest that even a small dose of meditation may improve attention and Focus when you're stressed out and time crunched. While practicing meditation may itself not feel relaxing or restful, the attention-performance improvements that come with it may still help you be more relaxed in general. Anyone who works in a high-pressure office environment should take heed of these findings.

Whac-a-Mole and Go with the Flow

As we've said, it makes perfect sense that mind wandering and daydreaming can lead to mistakes. But deep in the bowels of an Orlando, Florida warehouse, there lives a dusty, beady-eyed creature who personifies the upside of mind wandering for augmenting attentional control.

The creature, a hand-forged resin mole, is the last remaining remnant of the first Whac-a-Mole game. Its inventor, Aaron Fechter, says his inspiration for the game was an ill-conceived Japanese prototype he saw at a gaming convention in 1973. Fechter's original machine consisted of a large, waist-level cabinet with five holes in its top with each hole containing one mole and the air-powered device necessary to move it up and down. The object of the game was to wait for one of the moles to randomly pop up out of its hiding place and then smack it decisively on the head with a large, soft mallet. Whac-a-Mole is now a fixture at carnivals and gaming arcades all over the world, and though the mechanism has changed a bit and the moles are somewhat fancier, the gist of the game is pretty much the same.

You might think that the best strategy for playing Whac-a-Mole would be to stay vigilant and keenly focused so that as a mole peeks its head up, you're ready to strike. Not so. After thirty years of watching people play the game, Fechter swears he can tell how well someone is going to do the moment they step up to the mallet. "If they look alert and there's a lot of head and body movement, I know they're doomed," he says. "When they're loose and relaxed they usually get a high score."

Research backs Fechter up on this. In 2006, a team of Canadian researchers led by Dan Smilek studied the speed at which people were able to find a specific object among a bunch of similar objects—sort of like a video variation on Whac-a-Mole. Volunteers who were told to simply relax and allow the target to "pop up" in their mind scored higher than those who were told to actively scan for it. This suggests that a laid-back approach is sometimes faster and more efficient than active searching for a target. Smilek's team found that using a passive approach worked best when the search was hard, but not so well when the search was simple.

BE A WHAC-A-MOLE ZEN MASTER

Want to impress friends and family the next time the Whac-a-Mole game at the amusement park beckons? Take a few tips from Aaron Fechter, who claims he can rack up a perfect score every time he steps up to the mallet.

"The best way to get a high score is to gaze in a relaxed way at the center of the playing field with the side moles in your peripheral vision. At the start, hold your hammer over the center mole with it grazing the top of the mole's head. When the first mole pops up and you see where it is out of the corner of your eye, just swat at it—follow it with your eyes *but don't move your head at all*. After each swing, bring your mallet back to the center of the playing field and continue gazing and swatting, gazing and swatting. Do that and you'll hit practically every single one of those critters."

Fechter still plays Whac-a-Mole at conventions and arcades, stunning people with the ease with which he beats the game. They often say things like, "Wow, it's almost like you invented the game!" Fechter just puts the mallet down, smiles, and walks away. A Winner's Brain at work.

Of course, the act of relaxing your attention is used for higher purposes than searching for lost keys. As we mentioned in the last chapter on Motivation, letting go of your Focus while becoming fully immersed in what you are doing was described by psychologist Mihály Csíkszentmihályi as the state of *flow*, and it seems to be one of the keys to creativity. The octogenarian blues icon B. B. King describes what flow feels like: "When I'm doing improv, I seem to live what I'm doing in the moment. It's like playing a puzzle and every piece must fit. When you find those missing pieces it feels good, like a river flowing."

That "river flowing" is exactly what Charles Limb and Allen Braun were trying to capture in their fMRI scans of experienced jazz musicians at the National Institutes of Health MRI Facility in Bethesda, Maryland. They observed that the dorsolateral prefrontal cortex, which has been linked to planned actions and self-censoring, showed a slowdown in activity while the medial prefrontal cortex, which some scientists view as being critical for self-expression and individuality, showed increased activity. This may indeed be what happens in the brains of artists and non-artists alike when they let go and let their creative juices flow. And it's an ideal state for coming up with novel ideas and those lightbulb moments when you suddenly figure things out.

So, sometimes *not* focusing during idle moments gives us the solution to problems, allows us to make plans for the future, or gives us the chance to reflect on our selves. Indeed the same regions of the brain that are engaged when our minds wander are also key regions for helping us

Tranquil-Wiser

The take-home message here is to relax and be patient when Focus is key to the performance of a task, job, or skill. Push aside that hunt-it-down-and-kill-it intensity and simply relax and respond. The next time you're looking for your keys—something you may have had some practice doing—lighten up and let the brain do its thing without interference from the slower, more restricted, consciously controlled routines. Those slower, executive brain regions will switch off, allowing the relatively automatic, freely associative processes to take over.

to plan ahead, relate to others, anticipate future events, and predict what we might need to do to help us prepare for the future.

Anxiety results from situations where the challenge outpaces your ability and training—you become overfocused and unable to become immersed in the experience. Flow happens when there is a balance between level of ability (from talent, expertise, practice, training) and challenge (how difficult the activity is for you). And boredom results from situations where your ability and training exceed the challenge—there is no reward from excelling. So a tip for the Winner's Brain: Seek out situations that are challenging, and in which you can become immersed in what you are doing. Most people, through past experience and gut instinct, have a grasp of what types of interests keep them engaged.

You don't need to be an Olympic gymnast or fighter pilot to appreciate how finely tuned Focus skills can help you deal with life's constant distractions. Winner's Brains can shift to the right type of Focus for each situation, but they always try to prioritize information and stay locked on to what's important both in the moment and in the long term. Perhaps this chapter inspired you to take up yoga or meditation to help you hone your Focus skills (and as you shall see, they help augment many other Win Factors) or has shown you how you can reduce the demands on your Focus by practicing some parts of a skill until they are second nature. In the next chapter, you'll discover the key parts of the brain that are critically involved in balancing emotions and why they are so important for maintaining your Goal Laser, Opportunity Radar, and Optimal Risk Gauge.

Emotional Balance

Making Emotions Work in Your Favor

EMOTIONAL BALANCE

Winners recognize and anticipate emotional responses both in themselves and others so they can start, stop, and adjust emotions to fit any given situation.

Boost Your BrainPower: Emotional Balance is the aspect of Opportunity Radar that helps you manage your emotional responses when evaluating a situation. By not allowing your emotions to take over control of your brain, it keeps the beam on your Focus Laser steady. And it steadies your Risk Gauge by helping you contain your emotions when you decide to take a risk, especially when the risk doesn't pay off.

T HE INSULTS FLY at the small blond woman in the tank top like banana cream pies.

"Women are great drivers. Look at how many miles they get to the fender!"

"Baseball's for boys, honey. Go play with your Barbies!"

"Sweetie, why don't you try something you're good at—like the dishes!"

That last one hits home. She grabs a baseball and hurls it at a red metal circle. She misses, but after a dozen or so tries, the ball smacks the target and the obnoxious clown plunges into the large tank of water beneath him. She punches her fist in the air, and the crowd goes wild.

Who is the winner in this story? The woman "wins" because she gets to dunk the clown, but she blows a bundle of cash based on the taunts of some stranger in pancake makeup. On the other hand, the man behind the greasepaint, Terry Leonard, pulls in more than a hundred bucks an hour as a county fair Drown the Clown. "I make a pretty nice living by making people angry at me," Leonard laughs.

Angry, but not too angry. Good insult clowns know how to push people's buttons without pushing them over the edge. As Leonard astutely notes, "If they're not having fun, they're not spending money."

We bestow Winner's Brain status upon Leonard because he has a

Ph.D. level understanding of emotions, both his own and others. His Winner's Brain skill is Emotional Balance, the ability to consistently call upon the right emotion in the right dose at the right time to fit the circumstances.

People like Leonard have figured out that that *having* emotions is not the same thing as *balancing* emotions; in fact, Emotional Balance is the underpinning for many other Winner's Brain traits. Emotional strength is the oil that greases the gears of the recovery process (Resilience) whether you are going through a messy divorce, a sudden layoff, or any of the other tripwires you encounter in life. As for Talent Meter (the ability not only to be good at something, but also to recognize you're good at it), when you're tuned into the wrong emotional channel or you're continuously fiddling with the emotional dials, your Talent Meter gets about as good reception as a TV with tinfoil rabbit ears.

What Are Emotions, Anyway?

We think Emotional Balance is one of the most misunderstood Winner's Brain traits, perhaps because scientists and philosophers have debated for centuries, and are still debating, exactly what emotions are. We're with the growing number of experts who view emotions as a sliding scale of psychological responses ranging from pleasure at one end to displeasure at the other; these reactions allow us to assess the significance of everything we encounter—from events, to people, to even our own thoughts—with respect to our own needs and goals. This may sound like a somewhat detached and clinical explanation for something that rarely feels detached and clinical, but it actually does a pretty good job quantifying the subjective nature of feelings.

Not surprisingly, there is a direct link between the psychological aspects of emotions and the body's physiological response. This applies not only to voluntary responses but also to involuntary physical responses, a phenomenon frequently expressed in speech. Nervousness is described as butterflies in the stomach, excitement as a racing heart, fear as a knot in the gut. It is this primal connection between the physiological and physical that drives many of our actions and subsequent thoughts: *How you feel dictates how you react.*

All aspects of emotion are a result of specific brain activity, but until recently it was difficult to pinpoint exactly from which part of our neurocircuitry feelings originate. Now, thanks to modern technology, neuroscientists can show that emotions are generated in a network of brain structures, including regions of the anterior cingulate cortex, the orbitalfrontal region of prefrontal cortex directly above the eyes, and the insula, along with heavy involvement of the amygdala. A relatively common oversimplification equates the amygdala with emotion, but we now know that the processing of emotions is immensely complex. Nevertheless these compact clusters of cells in one of the most primitive parts of the brain do indeed contribute significantly to the elation you experience when you score tickets to a sold-out concert, and the disappointment you feel when you realize your seats are located directly behind a column. As you've read in other chapters, getting a handle on this small but mighty brain structure is the key to developing many Winner's Brain traits.

Winner's Brain Emotions

Every single person on the planet is programmed to feel emotions. It is impossible to erase them from the human experience. The difference between a Winner's Brain and an average brain is that Winners make a point of directing their emotions in productive ways. They don't simply spew out emotions in an uncontrolled or thoughtless manner; they are highly sensitive to their emotional responses (even the negative ones) so that emotions can make positive contributions to current and long-term goals. Maybe they don't always do this on a conscious level and maybe they can't pull off this magic trick every time, but largely, they are experts at channeling emotions productively, even when it is counterintuitive.

Our friend Ron, an FBI agent who has specialized in narcotics throughout his career, illustrates this point perfectly. He was once on a stakeout that involved busting up a ring of drug dealers. As he crouched in the bushes waiting for orders, he remembers feeling . . . relaxed.

Relaxed? Now, in everyday life, for the average person, this would be an ideal state of mind, but for an FBI agent in the midst of a drug bust, it can be an occupational hazard. In this scenario, controlled hyped-up and anxious feelings are the tools of the trade, the emotions Ron needed in order to stay focused. Now, as we wrote in the Focus chapter, relaxation can be a good thing, but this is one example where feeling too relaxed could be detrimental. As a matter of fact, Ron recalls having a conscious thought about how lives depended on his emotional state and making a deliberate effort to snap out of his complacency. At the same time he was careful not to slip too far to the other end of the emotional scale into outright jumpiness. "During a bust you want to get riled up but you don't want to see red," he explains.

What Ron intuitively grasped is that performance increases with emotional arousal, but only to a point. Not only is there an optimal emotional state for each situation, there is also an optimal emotional volume. This notion has evolved from what is now known as the Yerkes-Dodson law in honor of the two Harvard psychologists who first recognized the relationship between the intensity of stimulation and task performance.

As you can see on the next page, the relation between emotional arousal and performance forms an inverted U, where the upward part of the curve represents the positive energizing effect of arousal and the downward part represents the negative debilitating effects of arousal (or stress) on cognitive processes like attention, memory, and problem solving. As a seasoned FBI agent, Ron recognized that a certain level of aggression would serve him well because it would allow him to react if the

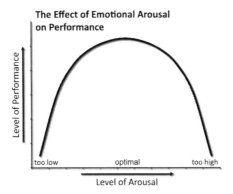

The Effect of Emotional Arousal on Performance

Level of Performance (vertical axis)

too low   optimal   too high

Level of Arousal

bust went bad. But if he cranked up the volume too far into the flashing red zone, he risked a sort of tunnel vision that would prevent him from accessing the logical, decision-making parts of his brain.

As we said, Ron's use of emotion may at first seem counterintuitive. It goes against the commonly held view that some feelings, like happiness and contentment, are always good whereas others, like anger and aggression, are always bad. He took emotions that are normally considered negative and directed them productively. His display of emotional control also dispels the misconception that, like waves upon the sand, emotions simply wash over you and there is nothing you can do about them. Although this is true with primitive feelings like the terror you would experience if you were trapped in a burning house, for the most part, you have the power to point your emotions in the direction of your goals.

Educating Yourself Emotionally

People like Ron probably have a natural propensity for emotional regulation, which they've enhanced through years of specialized training and experience. The good news is that Emotional Balance is a skill we can all improve upon. Like throwing a ball or learning how to drive, you get better with practice. It involves getting a handle on three fundamental concepts: recognizing emotions in yourself and others; predicting what emotional response you'll have in a given circumstance; and the art of adjusting your emotions accordingly to get what you want. This level of Emotional Balance carries with it quite a deep sense of Self-Awareness.

Recent work by Columbia University's Kevin Ochsner and his colleagues has explored whether or not we process our own emotions and the emotions of other people differently. By showing their volunteers a series of photos and then asking them to rate their own feelings or the feelings of the person in the photo, these researchers were able to establish that some of the same regions of the brain light up whether we are personally experiencing an emotion or judging someone else's experience. This demonstrates how heavily we rely on our own unique point of view to interpret the meaning of emotional status versus the actual, situational cues, regardless of whether we own the emotions or witness them in someone else.

Ochsner's findings speak directly to how a Winner's Brain succeeds in managing emotions. Most of us can read the primary colors of emotion. We know, for example, that an upturned mouth and laughing are associated with happiness, a downturned mouth and tears with unhappiness. Because Winners have such rich emotional pallets they can correctly decipher an untold number of subtle emotional colors, and this allows them to correctly assess their own emotional needs as well as the emotional needs of others.

Once you understand your emotions you can communicate them more clearly. If you're really good, you can express them through a puppet.

Elmo the Muppet appeared sporadically on *Sesame Street* for more than a decade before he was truly brought to life in 1984 by a talented young puppeteer named Kevin Clash. It is hard to imagine how such a large, handsome African-American man can make a small, furry red puppet come to life, yet that is exactly what happens. In Clash's hands, Elmo expresses joy, surprise, silliness, sadness, confusion, and an entire gamut

Taking Emotional Inventory Control

The first step toward learning Emotional Balance is "know thyself." Start by becoming more aware of your own personal emotional baseline, which is the normal range of your emotional responses including the highest highs and the lowest lows you typically achieve. (It's different for everybody.) Pay attention to your emotional comfort zones as well; try to determine which emotions seem to flow out of you easily and which are hard for you to express. Are you better expressing a range of happiness or sadness, satisfaction or anger? In Jeff's practice, he often recommends keeping a detailed emotional journal for a week or two to help strengthen your emotional vocabulary.

of sophisticated sentiments so well, even toddlers read them correctly. He doesn't do this with his falsetto voice alone (Clash's real voice is deep and smooth). With the arch of an eyebrow, the twitch of a paw, or sometimes just a straight look into the camera, he's able to telegraph his feelings better than many humans do.

"Successful puppeteers spend a lot of time observing people and we're very good at reading emotions and body language," Clash told us. "That's how we get these puppets to come to life."

Clash's knack for relating to the emotions of others allows him to channel a wide array of feelings through his fingertips, into Elmo, out through the camera and into the hearts and minds of his viewers. In Clash's line of work he has to deal with everyone from two-year-olds to A-list stars and he's great at it. Once, one of his mentors, master puppeteer Frank Oz, asked him to perform Miss Piggy in a movie and when Clash expressed doubt about being able to play the character, Oz told

Trading Places to Win

To cultivate a sense of empathy, try asking "What are you feeling?" instead of the typical "What are you thinking?" You can also get creative about compassion. Read books written for the opposite gender, a different nationality, or someone on the opposite side of the fence from you on an important social issue. Take a class meant for someone in a completely different profession. Anything that allows you to walk in someone else's emotional shoes will turn the dial up on Opportunity Radar by broadening your perspective, making you more aware of your abilities, and expanding your emotional range.

him, "Just imagine a trucker who always wanted to be a woman." Oz knew Clash was empathetic enough to translate those directions into a perfectly prissy pink pig!

If empathy is what makes Clash a great puppeteer, it's also what makes a nurse exceptional, a therapist effective, and someone a great parent. It's as essential to success as emotional Self-Awareness because it allows you to thrive in personal, professional, and social relationships.

Becoming an Emotional Prognosticator

Emotional responses are an important source of information and can have powerful effects on our decisions and behavior. Whether you know it or not, your decisions can be based on what you anticipate you're going to feel emotionally. A 2008 investigation by Julia Boehm and Sonja Lyubomirsky showed that you can literally "choose happiness" and that this choice often precedes success. They found that happy people earn more money, display superior performance, and perform more helpful acts compared to their more miserable peers. The evidence from this and other studies suggests not only that happiness correlates with workplace success but also that happiness often precedes it. What's in it for us? The accuracy of predicting emotional outcomes can either be a jackpot payoff or cost us emotional pain. The more accurate we become at predicting and guiding our emotional responses in different situations, the more easily we find joy, happiness, and other positive emotions. We can recognize when a situation will be worth the investment and when it won't.

Talented winners like Ilene Busch-Vishniac, a renowned researcher, inventor, and mechanical engineer, have a real knack for evaluating the potential returns on such emotional investments. As a woman in a male-centric part of academics, she has coped with the blatant inequalities she sometimes encounters. "I was once asked by the dean of a university to give my opinion regarding two candidates for the chair of my department," she recalls. "When I pointed out that there was an obvious third choice—me—and that I had been running the department for more than five years, he was absolutely baffled. He simply could not comprehend a woman department chair."

Though it was within her rights to feel bitter and angry—wouldn't you?—it was apparent to her that these emotions wouldn't help her win the chair position. Instead, she chose to view the situation calmly and rationally; ultimately this allowed her to take advantage of another Winner's Brain tool: Opportunity Radar. "When it's clear the glass ceiling is actually concrete, I simply look for opportunities elsewhere," she says.

She did look elsewhere. She is now the provost and vice president (academic) at McMaster University, one of Canada's most prestigious research and educational institutions. No barrier, be it made of glass, concrete, or any other material, can build a wall between someone like Busch-Vishniac and accomplishment. This is a trait most of us can cultivate far more than we may initially realize.

> You can plan to seek out or avoid specific situations based on the emotions you are trying to harness: Lonely? Make a lunch date with a friend. Depressed about your weight? Choose a route to work that avoids the bakery with the fattening cupcakes.

Managing Your Emotions

The crux of Emotional Balance is, of course, control. Not that we hold the view that emotions are damaging or something that should be entirely suppressed—they aren't and they can't be—but neither are they a raging tsunami over which you have no power. Led by researchers such as Ochsner and Stanford University's James Gross, the emerging field of emotion regulation explores how individuals influence which emotions they have, when they have them, and how they experience and express them. Gross and his colleagues believe you have five chances to influence your emotional reactions.

One of these chances comes when you decide which situations to put yourself in. This requires a level of emotional intelligence including a working knowledge of your emotional inventory, baselines, and comfort zones plus the ability to make reasonable predictions about which situations lead to which emotions. Some circumstances are unavoidable, but for the most part you have the power to choose, which opens up all sorts of possibilities for managing emotions.

If you find yourself in an emotionally charged situation despite your best efforts, you still have a shot at diffusing it by making an active, conscious effort to modify it. You might convert an inevitable meeting with an unpleasant client to a conference call to avoid a face-to-face, relax your jaw during a fight with your spouse, or calmly ask a neighbor to tone down a raucous party.

Build Bookends

Say you are about to give a presentation at an important meeting—but you need to get your car inspected by the end of the day, you're late for work, and there's a stack of bills piling up on your desk. Try something psychologists call "bookending," an effective technique when you're under a lot of stress or in the midst of a "worry spiral" but you still need to be productive.

Kerri Strug famously nailed the winning vault at the 1996 Olympics despite severely injuring her ankle on her previous attempt. Rather than getting caught up in the moment, she bookended, blocking out everything about a stressful event except one manageable task—in her case, the Yurchenko 1½ twist. "I didn't hear the crowd or think about my ankle or what was riding on my success or failure," she told us. "I just concentrated on my performance."

Try using a cue word like "now" that acts as a bookend: This is the point where you put everything else on the other side of the wall and concentrate exclusively on your presentation. Afterwards you can lift that bookend and put a bookend on another task like, say, getting your car inspected.

And if that doesn't work or isn't appropriate, try creating a distraction. As a kid, did you cover your eyes or turn away from the screen when you watched a scary movie? You were doing something psychologists call attentional deployment—directing your attention away from a too-intense emotional event. B. B. King told us that he did not like it when fights broke out during his concerts (Hey, would you like it if a fistfight broke out at your office?) so when he saw trouble brewing, he played something upbeat to change the mood of the crowd. By distracting someone about to throw a punch with happy music, he pulls off an emotional sleight of hand. In simplistic brain science terms, he diverted the emotional part of the brain with the attentional part of the brain.

You also have the option of changing your perspective. When your boss gives you extra work, you have two choices: You can either feel put upon and overloaded or you can feel good that your boss gives you so much work because he trusts you'll get the job done. Studies such as that conducted at the University of Chicago by Sarah Banks and colleagues support our belief that this process of reframing, sometimes called reappraisal, leads to improved brain-function connectivity between specific areas of the frontal cortex and the emotion-related amygdala. Other studies, such as that by Jane Richards and Gross, suggest that reframing can actually relieve the cognitive demands your brain faces otherwise when coping with emotional events. They found that those who reframe a highly emotional event by working through the issues beforehand until they view them as challenges rather than problems are able to remain calmer and have a better memory for the details than those who stress out or try to suppress their feelings.

Finally, if all else fails, reach into your emotional bag of tricks one last time and do what your mother always told you to do when you were upset or angry: Take a deep breath.

Emotions can either be a banana-cream pie in the face or a productive set of tools for helping you advance toward your goals. The brain's emotional responses aren't exclusively positive or negative; the balance of power between different brain regions allows you to customize your emotions to be appropriate for each particular situation. By understanding how you experience emotions and how others react emotionally to you, you can strive toward effective Emotional Balance. As you'll read about next, a Winner's Brain has a well-developed system in support of the Memory Win Factor, which can help you anticipate the curves in the road you'll encounter on the way to success and up the wattage on all of your BrainPower Tools in the process.

Memory

"Remembering" to Have
a Winner's Brain

MEMORY

Winner's Brains don't just store a lot of information in memory—they apply their past experience and use it to strategically build new knowledge in order to improve future performance.

Boost Your BrainPower: Is there a BrainPower Tool that doesn't rely on Memory? Opportunity Radar and Optimal Risk Gauge, for instance, draw upon past experience in order to evaluate similar circumstances. The fact is, almost everything we do is based on evaluating past experience in order to predict the future.

I N THE PROCESS OF WRITING THIS BOOK, Mark shot an unarmed man. It was all in the name of gaining better insight into what makes a Winner's Brain tick.

Of course, he didn't actually shoot bullets into a live person. The gun was real enough, but it was hooked up by a long black cable to a virtual reality machine controlled by Special Agent Keith H., our FBI firearms training instructor. Keith first strapped a gun holster onto Mark's belt, then projected a video of a raid on a suspected bank robber's apartment onto a large screen. Once the video scenario started rolling, Keith used a remote control mounted onto a large console to key in the action. Depending upon how Mark reacted, Keith shifted the scenario to introduce a series of twists and turns to the plot.

Unfortunately, Mark did not react well. Rapid gunfire filled the air as Mark shot the suspect multiple times in the head, legs, and chest, even though the suspect had raised his hands up in surrender and was backed into a corner. Mark was also completely oblivious when the suspect's petite girlfriend drew a pistol from the back of her pants and popped off several rounds.

By the way, no smugness out of Liz or Jeff here, who also attempted the same virtual reality scenario. In the course of her raid, Liz seriously wounded a 12-year-old boy, and in his, Jeff killed a fellow FBI agent.

Memory Is All in Your Head

Before we entered the office-sized virtual reality room, clipped the decommissioned revolver onto our belts, and faced the video screen, we had immersed ourselves in two days of intensive training at the FBI Academy delivered by their top instructors. Besides Keith, principal Firearms Instructor at Quantico, there was Ron, an ex-navy Seal, and, Clay, who had formerly operated the reactor aboard a navy nuclear submarine. We originally contacted Keith about doing a straightforward interview for this book, but when he generously invited us to Quantico to experience some of the FBI's critical field training for ourselves we thought, why not? What better way to absorb the Winner's Brain mentality it takes to be a successful agent than to try it firsthand? All three of us practically jumped on the first plane to Virginia.

Our training involved several hours in the FBI's cavernous shooting range learning proper technique, gun safety protocol, and shooting strategy. We visited Hogan's Alley, the gritty-but-fake town that is used to drill agents in training by re-creating shootouts, raids, and any number of other sticky situations. There, Keith and company drilled us on things like how to see bad guys before they see you, making split-second decisions, and using the other guy's response to your advantage, all of which we practiced over and over again for nearly half a day.

By the end of our Gunfighter University immersion course, we had received a rather complete education on the appropriate use of force and how to respond in do-or-die situations involving guns and violence. Copious amounts of information had been drilled into our brains. Any one of us would have aced the written.

And yet, when the lights dimmed . . . brain freeze all around.

Now, we could have related this story as part of the Emotional Balance chapter—there is certainly a great deal of emotional control required to properly handle a firearm in the face of a threat. Or perhaps within the Focus or Self-Awareness chapter—both these Win Factors are important in such a scenario too. But we tell it here to illustrate just how fragile Memory can be and how inextricably bound it is with so many other Winner's Brain traits. Most Memory improvement methods emphasize how to get information into your brain and keep it there, just so you can regurgitate it later. But they don't take into account that you may be required to access these memories later in emotionally charged situations, such as when you are nervous about speaking to a large group of people or you're a contestant on a quiz show seen by millions of people or when there are bullets whizzing past your head.

We've elected to present a different take on Memory than many pop culture approaches: We emphasize the ability to access memories in the real world. In many ways, Memory is what makes you uniquely you. You are, after all, the sum of your remembered experiences. But a Winner's Brain doesn't simply store data like an old computer disk. It emphasizes quality over quantity.

Shooting from the Hippocampus

The human brain has an impressive capacity for remembering things. At around 18 months, for instance, toddlers begin an astonishing language explosion, learning and retaining the meaning of up to 10 words per day. By the time we reach adulthood, most of us recognize at least 60,000 words. Add to this hundreds of thousands of other experiences and skills like the driving route from home to work, plus the scent of roses in your neighbor's garden when you were ten, plus the taste of lemons, plus the sound of an out-of-tune piano, plus the first time you met your spouse, plus how to throw a ball, plus the satisfaction you feel when you win a tennis match—and it's clear the brain must have some sort of massive mental storage closet for information.

In fact, the brain has numerous storage closets (and retrieval systems) for many different types of memories. When information arrives in your brain, it is first routed through to the appropriate sensory areas. What you see goes to the visual cortex in the occipital lobe, what you hear goes to the auditory cortex in the temporal lobe, what you taste goes to the insular-opercular cortex, and so on, then rerouted to other neural destinations as your brain works to recognize and evaluate the incoming information. After a day at the beach, your memories of the smell of sunscreen, the blueness of the sky, the sound of waves crashing against the shore, and the feel of sand beneath your feet are all distributed to the various areas of your brain responsible for storage of that specific type of information. As involved as the process sounds, the neural firing and communication involved typically take only a fraction of a second.

A key structure that weaves these various Memory traces into a unified experience is the hippocampus, a large curved structure buried deep within the temporal lobe on each side of the brain. The hippocampus and adjacent areas of the medial temporal lobe work closely with other regions such as the amygdala and prefrontal cortex to evaluate the importance of incoming information. Data you don't need may seem to evaporate into the ether, while relevant data are consolidated into long-term storage for possible future use.

Of our first stint at the firing range, Mark can recall the feel of his finger pulling the trigger and the movement of the gun when the bullet left the chamber because parts of his brain encoded that information as something that might come in handy at some later point. He has no memory of what Keith was wearing or where Jeff was standing at the time because this information was peripheral and insignificant to the demands placed on his brain at the time.

When you need a memory, your brain gathers the various bits and pieces like the ingredients of a recipe, stirs them together, and pours them back in your working memory. The prefrontal cortex acts as the de facto head chef, recruiting the various parts of the brain needed to both recall the memory and put it to use. This head chef's role is critical because the process of making and later reconstructing a memory isn't a consistent one. A memory can be influenced by mood, surroundings, and other circumstances, both at the time it was formed and later when it's recalled. For example, you tend to encode memories more strongly when you are in a highly emotional state, it has significant meaning, it's really unusual, or you're paying close attention. The same is true of recall, which is why, as with any recipe, a memory may be a little different each time you remember it.

Constructing a Proactive Brain

Russian-born Mark Bluvshtein began playing chess at the age of five. At age 11 his family moved to Toronto, and at the age of 16, he became the youngest Canadian grandmaster chess player in history.

As Bluvshtein, now 21, will attest, being a world-class chess player requires sharp mental skills, with a great memory chief among them. "I have a chessboard in my head so I don't actually need to look at the board in front of me to see the pieces moving and think six moves ahead," he explained to us. "It's like I grow a tree from my memory and all the possible variations are the branches."

This is an excellent illustration of what, in 2007, Harvard Medical School researcher Moshe Bar referred to as the proactive brain (and part of what gives Bluvshtein a Winner's Brain). "Most people view memory like it's a videotape or a photo album containing all of your life experiences," Bar told us. "But really it's there to directly influence the present moment and the way you perceive and interact with your environment."

The current speculation of researchers like Bar is that the brain relies on memory to imagine, simulate, and predict possible future events. Indeed, a rapidly growing number of studies show that imagining the future depends on much of the same neural machinery that is needed for

Try Something New

Some brains are more proactive than others. One of the best ways to take your use of memory to a higher level is by exposing it to as many new experiences as possible. Recent fMRI studies conducted in Magdeburg, Germany, by Björn Schott and colleagues demonstrate how novelty stimulates activity not only in the memory centers of the hippocampus/medial temporal lobe but also in the dopamine-rich midbrain areas responsible for Motivation and reward processing. Because dopamine can enhance learning, anything you consider unique gives your proactive neurocircuitry more ammunition.

So aim to try something new and different at least once a week. It doesn't have to be on a grand scale like taking a trip or parachuting out of a plane (although those things certainly qualify); even something as small as tasting an exotic new fruit, learning the meaning of a few new words, or trying out a new soap provides you with more cross reference material for the future. With each new experience, trust your brain to store the information, integrate it into what's already there, and pull it out when needed.

remembering the past. Bluvshtein's proactive brain therefore allows him to make accurate predictions about where a game is going based upon recollection of previous games. Recalling the rarely used king's gambit at the Montreal International in 2007, for example, allowed him to anticipate his opponent's opening move and the series of moves that came next, and thus enabled him to defend his position perfectly and score a counterattack for the win.

In many ways, the gift of prediction is memory's most crucial contribution to success. While stuffing information into memory can make life less frustrating and more productive by reducing the time you spend

Prime Your Brain

Bar also says that even straightforward memory functions like memorizing a grocery list can be improved using a proactive approach: "If you scan the list just as you enter the market, things will pop out at you because you have primed the brain. Seeing the list-items becomes a prediction in a sense." The advantage to this method compared to a more rigid memorization system or the hard copy list is that you can simply walk the supermarket aisles grabbing things you need rather than having to retrace your steps as the items are recalled in order. For example, once you have scanned the list, your brain will generate signals related to a jar of mayonnaise, cold cuts, pasta, and so on. "These things will stand out on the shelf compared to things your brain hasn't 'predicted,'" Bar says.

hunting for your car keys or preventing extra trips to the market to buy the milk you forgot, it doesn't go beyond the simple maintenance of information. The advantage of being able to see six moves ahead, whether on a chessboard or in life, is that you consider the consequences of your potential actions and adjust your strategy accordingly.

Making Memories Durable

Some memories are embedded in your brain like rocks while others fade like watercolors. Durable memory is particularly helpful for recalling lists, names, and phone numbers. A Winner's Brain capitalizes on ways to purposely strengthen memory traces for important information to ensure that it can be efficiently retrieved when it is most needed.

One way to make a memory more forget-proof is to attach it to something already familiar. Boston University memory researcher Elizabeth Kensinger explained to us that the way information is initially processed can influence the likelihood that it becomes stored in a more durable format. "When new information is connected to existing knowledge or when you concentrate on the meaning of that information," she told us, "you are more likely to retain it in memory."

Kensinger says that this type of mental journey into the corners of your mind works because of the specific regions of prefrontal cortex that become involved—areas that are particularly active during the type of flexible thinking that allows you to connect the meaning of information with something already familiar to you. "When you engage these regions, you are more likely to encode information deeply," Kensinger explains. In 2009, two different research teams, one in Japan led by Yumiko Kondo and another in Britain led by Daniel Bor, confirmed this in separate fMRI studies.

Practice is another way to increase the strength of a memory. Though novelty is important for building a more prospective brain, repetition is also important, especially for information that is routinized and especially if you need to call upon the routine under pressure. Practice allows your brain to expend less effort when it retrieves and processes critical information so it is able to do so more quickly and automatically.

This was certainly true for veteran firefighter John Morabito on the morning of September 11, 2001, when terrorists crashed two jets into the World Trade Center towers. He was just coming on shift at Ladder 10, the closest firehouse to the towers, when the first plane hit. As he sprinted toward the burning buildings and later as he raced away from them just seconds before they collapsed, he remembers feeling overwhelmed with emotion. But Morabito has a Winner's Brain—and he's possibly a Superhero. Even as debris and bodies were falling from the sky all around him, he was able to save not only himself but hundreds of other people too. Relying on skills and abilities learned through his ex-

The Journey Technique

Although we've purposely avoided bombarding you with standard memory tricks, one very effective way to anchor a memory is with a method that was used by the ancient Greeks called the *journey technique* or *the method of loci*. Start by mentally picturing a familiar journey, and placing pictures associated to the information you are trying to memorize along that route. Then when remembering the information, you simply go on your mental journey and "pick up" all of the things you placed there.

For example, you can translate numbers into images that resemble their shape; the number one becomes a candle, the number two becomes a snake, the number three becomes a camel's humps, etc. To help remember the bank pin of 1580, you can imagine walking into a bank carrying a candle (1), standing in line behind a seahorse (5), and seeing a snowman (8) bouncing a football (0) behind the counter.

tensive training and past experience allowed him to stay focused and keep his cool.

New York City firefighters receive over 600 hours of training and a multitude of written exams before they are eligible for assignment. By the time they encounter their first fire, a lot of what they need to do is so practiced and ingrained they could practically perform their job in their sleep. Even inexperienced firefighters are "experienced," and the longer they stay on the job, the more training and experience they get. This is no different from FBI agents like Keith (650 hours of training), pilots like Geoff Billingsley (up to 2,000 hours of training), doctors (an average of 11 years), and many others in professions that call for performance under pressure. According to fMRI studies at UCLA led by Russell Poldrack, the more extensive the practice, the more automatic the task because it reduces the need for deliberate control over performance by the lateral prefrontal cortex and increases activity in regions of the basal ganglia, a subcortical structure critically involved in training-related skill acquisition.

Also, no one ever said a memory has to be real in order to help you gain practice. While in training Geoff Billingsley would sit in a chair, toilet plunger between his knees, pretending to fly a real plane. He logged hundreds of chair-flying hours before he ever set foot in a cockpit. By the time he took flight, many of the basic controls and commands were second nature to him despite the fact he had never actually flown a plane.

A mentally simulated experience can sometimes serve the purpose just as well as a real one. Think of it as a mental dress rehearsal for the real deal, sort of like taking as many do-overs as you'd like, with none of the consequences for making mistakes. Start by closing your eyes and visualizing the scenario you want to rehearse. Say, for instance, you are about to go on a job interview. Lead yourself through all of the possibilities of what might go well and what might go wrong. Try to focus all of your senses, not just sight or sound. Although Bar says imagined scenarios don't have as much depth as real-life experiences, you can get close and you will get better with practice.

A third way that memories can be made more durable is to form them under highly emotional circumstances. Kensinger and Harvard memory expert Dan Schacter did a 2006 survey of Yankees and Red Sox fans and found that those who viewed the outcome of the final game of the 2004 American League championships (when the Sox clinched the pennant) either very positively or very negatively were more likely to recall specific details about the game and their own surroundings compared to those who weren't all that invested, but their memories were no more accurate than those of the cooler fans. Their research converges with classic research by two other Harvard psychologists, Roger Brown and James

Practice Makes Perfect Memory

So if you need to recall a particular sequence of information—whether it is because you need to use it often or because it is very important to get it right—drill it until it becomes second nature. This is especially true if you are expected to perform under stress. For instance, what is more stressful (in a good way) than a wedding? There are often several dress rehearsals a few days leading up to the big event where the entire bridal party practices walking down the aisle, memorizing the order everyone enters, where they stand and what they say. All of this is to minimize the chance of a nervous bride tripping over her wedding dress or an anxious groom forgetting his vows. Whenever possible, practice the task in the same or similar place you will ultimately perform it; if that isn't possible, visualization can also be very effective at helping you prepare.

Kulik, on what they termed flashbulb memories because of the highly detailed, frozen-snapshot-in-time impression that surprising, emotionally arousing, or otherwise personally significant events tend to leave. Brown and Kulik found that events of this kind were often recalled with distinctive clarity, even some time after the event. Whether the details are about a momentous ball game or, in the case of the Brown and Kulick's research, what participants remember from when they found out that President John F. Kennedy had been shot, such studies show that highly emotional experiences are often remembered more richly than those for emotionally neutral events.

John Morabito's memories of September 11, 2001, are another good example of this phenomenon; they are as crisp and clear as the sky before smoke and fire turned it black. He recalls details such as the hair color of a woman he saved, an expression on his captain's face, and the temperature of the glass of water he was drinking when he looked up and saw his brother, who is also a firefighter, five hours after he had been reported as missing and presumed dead. Perhaps most poignant is his description of what it was like right after the towers collapsed. "It was like a nuclear winter with smoke and dust everywhere. The sky and air just vanished," he says. His heightened emotional state caused his memories to imprint deeply. He probably can't recall the temperature of any other glass of water he drank during that decade.

Yet of these three methods, injecting emotion into a situation is probably the least reliable way to create durable memories since even the most emotionally balanced person doesn't always have control over what they are feeling at the time a memory is formed. We mention it here because you should be aware how profoundly emotion affects memory. The more emotionally charged the moment (especially when that emotion is stress or fear), the more profound the effect on memory. As Kensinger and Schacter's sports-fan survey showed, their most emotional subjects were also the most adamant about what they remembered, but not necessarily any more accurate in their recall than non-emotional subjects. Winner's Brains are certainly not immune to this phenomenon, but they are more aware that this is the case.

GET THE POINT

In 2007, a team of scientists led by the University of Rochester's Susan Cook were trying to find a way of helping middle school children learn some tricky algebra concepts when they hit upon a simple memory aid: Pointing.

More than 90 percent of the students who gestured to an algebraic problem while trying to learn it remembered the information three weeks later whether or not they reviewed it verbally, compared to just 33 percent of students who merely talked through the solution. The researchers speculated that gesturing makes memories more durable because it taps into the human need to experience, capitalizing on our desire to interact with our environment.

Though more research is needed to understand why and which parts of the brain latch onto gestures and attach them to memories, we suspect this theory has merit from interviewing so many Winner's Brains whose memories and brains work closely together. Laura Linney told us that how she uses her body is just as important as the words she speaks in building a memorable character. And Phyllis Diller says her body language sells the joke just as much as the joke itself. Study for yourself which gestures you use that seem to make the most powerful impact.

Forget About It

And while creating those rock-solid durable memories is an important Winner's Brain skill, Kensinger points out that diluting some memories is equally important. "Selectivity probably makes it easier for us to conjure up memories that are relevant to our current thoughts and actions without having to rummage through too much useless brain clutter," she told us.

A 2008 fMRI study led by New Jersey research scientist Glenn R. Wylie demonstrated that such intentional forgetting works; the researchers found less evidence that items shown in a study session were encoded into memory for items that participants actively tried to forget than those that they tried to remember. The results of the study also suggest that actively forgetting something recruits frontal regions associated

Edit Your Brain

You can actively and consciously purge information you don't need from your brain. Imagine a broom sweeping away useless information like the answers to a test or an old phone number. Whenever the information pops up into your head, pick up your mental dustpan and sweep it into the trash. You may also clear the information clutter on the front end, much as you cut the fat away from the meat before you cook it. If you learn to recognize the information you don't need up front, you can discard it immediately in order to concentrate on the more substantive information.

with controlling thoughts and also showed a boosted signal to the hippocampus, when compared to instances of standard, passive forgetting.

What Is Déjà Vu? What Is Déjà Vu?

Anyone who's had déjà vu is familiar with that slightly creepy feeling that history is repeating itself. It's one of the strangest sensations a person can have.

What causes you to return to the past that's never actually happened? No one knows for sure, but the most plausible explanation seems to be a mix-up in your brain's memory process; when parts of a new situation are very similar to some prior experience, the fluency with which the brain processes the relevant elements seems to elicit strong feelings of familiarity. The resulting experience can make you feel like you've stumbled into the movie *Groundhog Day*.

About ten percent of people say they experience déjà vu often, but about the same percentage report never having it at all. Most people have their first encounter with it at around age eight or nine, and everyone is more susceptible when stressed or tired. As you get older, you tend to take fewer of these false trips down memory lane. Anything can trigger it. Just reading these words for instance . . . Wait, haven't you read this before?

This chapter showed how the brain is configured to maximize future performance based upon past experience and how many other Win Factors (such as Emotional Balance and Focus) are involved in this process. Memory's most important function is to help you make predictions about the future so you can make accurate conclusions about how to best achieve your goals. New experiences can help enhance the impact of your memory by giving the underlying neural mechanisms more information to draw upon when making decisions in the future. Next up: How a Winner's Brain deals with adversity, and how becoming more resilient can help you bounce back from whatever life throws at you.

Resilience

Bouncing Back into Success

RESILIENCE

The art of bounce: A Winner's Brain recovers from life's challenges by dealing with shortcomings, misfires, and failures whether they are self-generated or brought on by circumstances beyond one's control. Winners reframe failures so that they work to their advantage and recognize that when things don't go according to plan the journey isn't necessarily over—and in fact failure is often a new opportunity in disguise.

Boost Your BrainPower: Effort Accelerator, Goal Laser, Talent Meter. Having good Resilience skills keeps your Effort Accelerator going even when the going gets tough. Resilience also means that you don't give up on your goals when you have a setback or doubt your talents when you don't get what you want every time.

N|O ONE SKATES THROUGH LIFE without coming up against a few challenges. For the most part, we're faced with minor speed bumps. But some life events, like a messy divorce or financial ruin, can turn out to be major stumbling blocks. The ability to recover from the bad stuff and move forward with your head held high is a trait we call Resilience. Possessing strong Resilience skills is a key Winner's Brain strategy.

Just listen to what Whoopi Goldberg, the Queen of Resilience, told us about bouncing back from misfortune: "You say to yourself it's bad but what do I do? Is it so bad I can't get up? Is it so bad nothing else matters in the world? When the newspapers are always talking about you, you could stay in bed all day from it. I've made the decision to get up and keep on going no matter what."

Goldberg, daughter of a single mom, grew up poor in a New York City housing project. She's lived through three divorces, her daughter's teenage pregnancy, and more highly publicized flops and failures than she cares to count. She's on a first-name basis with adversity, yet seems to weather each storm relatively unscathed and largely unruffled. She attributes this wonderful capacity for rebound to her mother, who taught her she shouldn't simply lie down and die in the face of a crisis. "If you do you're dead. That's pretty finite," she told us in her trademark wry and understated way.

Whoopi's right. Resilience is one of life's lessons that *can* be learned along the way. While some aspects of Resilience are wired into the brain from the start, emerging science tells us that it can also be developed. Battling adversity is something you can intentionally practice and get better at.

This Is Your Brain Being Resilient

If you were to catch someone's brain in the act of experiencing adversity, you'd see a flurry of activity in three primary (and, by now, highly familiar!) locations: the amygdala, insula, and anterior cingulate cortex. The amygdala is tucked deep within the temporal lobe of each side of the brain. Along with other parts of the limbic system, it's responsible for most of our primal emotional responses like happiness, fear, and disgust. The insula, despite belonging to the more recently evolved and infinitely more rational cerebral cortex, is a major player in many of our visceral gut reactions. Thank the insula for those feelings of revulsion the next time you discover rotting, moldy chicken hidden in the back of your refrigerator. The anterior cingulate cortex is a central region in the frontal lobe. It plays a role in a lot of Winner's Brain traits, and in the case of Resilience, its role is to spot errors and conflicts as they occur and help other areas of the brain regulate your emotional response to them.

On those occasions when the brain perceives that things are not going so well, the sparks start flying in all three of these areas. Recent fMRI experiments have been able to watch this phenomenon unfold so we know this is how virtually every normally functioning brain reacts to failure. It's what happens next that sets the Winner's Brain apart from the brain that is average.

A 2008 study conducted by Christian Waugh and colleagues at the University of Michigan was one of the first to capture the nuances of how Resilience emerges from the brain. The scientists began by administering a series of psychological tests to volunteers in order to categorize them as either high-resilience or low-resilience people. Next, they flashed a series of images onto a video screen in the MRI scanner and measured the subjects' brain activity. The researchers were most interested in seeing what happened when the individuals were exposed to revolting things like overflowing toilets and spoiled food (standardized research images, which, by the way, have caused many a scientist to gag when selecting them to use). Before viewing each picture, the subjects were given a cue that let them know the chances of seeing either a disgusting or neutral image.

As expected, regardless of Resilience rating, all the subjects' brain crisis centers went into overdrive whenever the cues hinted at the possibility they might be subjected to one of those disgusting images. But the high-resilients and low-resilients parted company whenever the picture turned out to be neutral after all. High-resilience subjects were able to disengage these emotion centers, especially the insula, but low-resilience individuals remained keyed up, with prolonged activation of these regions for some time after. This simply means the highly resilient brains were able to temper their emotional response following a potential threat and had the ability to quickly recover when everything turned out all right. Low-resilience brains weren't able to dial down their activity, especially in the reactive insula, even when no threat materialized.

So does this mean that if you're currently the owner of a low-resilience brain, you're destined to feel paralyzed or wallow in self-pity every time you suffer a setback? No. With practice you can actually control brain activity to help modify your response to disappointment and failure. This is what Andrea Caria and colleagues found in their 2007 study when they used real-time fMRI scans to show participants in Tübingen, Germany, how their brains responded to making a mistake on a task. By viewing their brain activity at the instant they made an error, subjects learned the art of insular control—and thus emotional control—in just three four-minute sessions. Based on this type of cutting-edge research and our own clinical experience, we believe it is possible to improve your ability to weather adversity and failures by using the strategies we describe in this chapter, no matter how you've reacted to misfortune in the past.

Learn to Play the Odds

Suzanne Schlosberg tried a lot of different ways to meet men before she finally married in 2003. She even tried speed dating—that late 20th-century twist on the old-fashioned tradition of matchmaking. Schlosberg describes how it works: "You sit in a large room and do a round robin with 20 or so perspective suitors, chatting with each for about three minutes before they move to another table. At the end of each 'date' both of you check off a form that says whether or not you're interested in seeing the person again and hopefully, you wind up the evening being compatible with at least one person."

In a way, speed dating is based on the concept of lowering your expectations. You willingly tolerate up to 19 failures in the hopes of realizing just one success. It's a perfect metaphor for how you can fortify your Resilience to failure in everyday life. Think about it. Even the greatest hitters in baseball only get a hit a third of the time. The average smoker tries to quit eight times before actually kicking the habit. Daters, hitters, and quitters are still successful, too.

Studies support the efficacy of this speed-dating approach to Resilience. A study conducted in Diego Pizzagalli's Harvard-based Affective Neuroscience Laboratory suggests that those who tolerate mistakes show lower activity in the anterior cingulate cortex—the part of the brain that is responsible for monitoring conflicts among different brain signals

Loss Opportunities

Failure is an expected milestone on the path to success. Failing does *not* mean you can never succeed, it just means you don't succeed every time. When you practice anticipating and accepting failure without fear or judgment, you leave the door open for success.

One way to deal with a mistake is to simply block it from your mind. In most cases one error isn't a deal breaker, so blocking out the error and immediately refocusing attention on the next performance can keep you from blowing one slip-up out of proportion. By doing this while taking a test, for example, you avoid the common problem of letting one answer you don't know derail your performance on the entire exam. Studies show the success of this strategy is reflected by the direct effects it has on the activity of that oh-so-temperamental anterior cingulate cortex.

and that processes the significance of emotional events—and are able to move on to the next task far more easily than those who don't tolerate their mistakes very well. In fact, those who become overly upset by the errors they make—i.e., failures—may experience more symptoms of anxiety and depression than others.

Grab the Wheel

In 1954, psychologist Julian Rotter coined the term "locus of control" to refer to people's belief about what causes good and bad things to happen in their lives. An internal locus of control reflects the belief that you are master of your own destiny; an external locus of control reflects just the

Electing Your Perspective

If you're a card-carrying member of the external locus of control club, you can change your worldview by facing up to the realization, then committing to the belief that you have an active role in deciding your own fate. It isn't always easy, and Rotter has counseled hundreds of externals to work first on the small things you always tell yourself you don't have the power to change—but really, you do. For example, if you're out of work you can sit there and wait for the phone to ring—or you can hit the pavement to personally hand your résumé to prospective employers. Obviously, the proactive internal approach to job hunting is more likely to get results than the passive, external approach, but externals often cannot imagine taking such steps.

Once you gain confidence with smaller acts of control, you can gradually work up to facing the larger challenges in your life with a more take-charge attitude. Try to think of failure as a trampoline: Each time you rebound, you build more momentum. The next bounce might lead to success.

opposite. Externals believe events happen because an outside force like the environment, another person, or a higher power is calling the shots and that there is very little they can do about it.

When you have an internal locus of control like Trisha Meili, you "grab the wheel" of life. As she recovered from that terrible attack in Central Park, media reports said she'd see improvements for a year or two, but after that she'd reach a plateau and probably never be able to live on her own again.

When Meili heard these reports, she remembers thinking, "Don't count me out." And, of course, she proved everyone wrong. She made a full recovery and has gone on to an inspiring career as a motivational speaker who delivers what she calls "a message of hope and possibility." She told us that from the moment she came out of six weeks of coma and delirium, she was determined to reclaim her life, refusing to get caught up in a past she couldn't change.

Meili isn't sure she has always been so self-determined, but she believes her tragedy has given her a great faith in herself and in her own ability to succeed. Rotter would define this as a classic internal locus of control mentality. "Internals bounce back because they expect to bounce back," he told us. "Externals are constantly looking back. They blame everything on luck. Eventually they just give up because they find it too hard to go on."

Your Performance Will Never Exceed Your Self-Image

"My fat mother-in-law went to the doctor with a pain in her left breast . . . It turned out to be a trick knee." This is the joke comic pioneer Phyllis Diller tells us to illustrate a point.

Night after night she would tell this joke, and it would fall flat. But even as a young comic just starting out, Diller had a lot of self-confidence and a strong self-image. A more cowardly performer might have cut the line, but she *knew* it was funny. (Admit it, you laughed.) "After a few shows, I realized it was too close to the other lines about her being fat so I took it and put it with the eating lines and it killed," she told us, laughing that unmistakable staccato laugh of hers.

Diller knew instinctively she had much to learn from the performances where she bombed. Instead of slinking offstage with her tail between her legs, she stayed focused and positive. She kept tinkering with her act until she felt she had finally gotten it right—and when she did, the audience responded. She's earned her Ph.D. in failure by studying and dissecting her flops in order to tease out the elements of the situation that worked and the ones that didn't. She learned that sometimes you have to take a big leap outside your comfort zone and be willing to take a few blows to the old ego before you achieve your goals. You can do it too.

Successful people are able to slow down following an error, just enough to alter their behavior and avoid another mistake. Studies conducted by Michael Robinson at North Dakota State University associated this ability to step on the failure brakes after making a mistake—or alternatively, step on the accelerator when you are correct—with a superior ability to understand your own motives and experience a higher level of satisfaction and well-being.

So after you make a blunder or you've experienced a personal setback, slow down for a moment, take a deep breath, and consciously try to determine the source of your mistake. Once you find it, adjust your behavior accordingly, put it in the past, and get moving again!

Find a Failure Role Model

To mix metaphors, successful people don't jump ship just before it docks. There are plenty of examples throughout this book of individuals who experienced quite a bit of failure before they achieved their goals. People like Elizabeth Hudson, whom you met in the Self-Awareness chapter. She was able to break away from a life of drug addiction and prostitution to become a mom and a notable author. Whoopi Goldberg and B. B. King grew up amid poverty and prejudice, but they were still able to build incredibly successful careers as entertainers. Think of these people as Resilience role models.

Resilience role models demonstrate how common it is to encounter obstacles on the road to success. You probably don't have to think very hard to come up with a few Resilience role models you know personally. Either by instinct or training, these people implement many of the techniques we suggest in this chapter to bounce back from adversity.

Learning from Other People's Mistakes

The next time the chips are down, ask yourself, "What would a favorite professor, boss, parent, or movie action hero do?" By identifying a Resilience role model, you'll be able to draw on more than just your own thoughts and coping resources. Try reaching out for a helping hand. You can also keep company with like-minded people as a way to meet resilience role models. You can find strength and support just by listening to the war stories of others who've fallen short of their goals and then have gone on to succeed.

In counseling sessions, Dr. Jeff Brown often tells patients who are having trouble getting past a crisis to ask themselves what advice their role model would give. This works thanks to a network of specialized brain cells called mirror neurons that run throughout different parts of the brain. As we mentioned in the Self-Awareness chapter, you can think of these as your "monkey see, monkey do" brain cells for their ability to provide a kind of inner imitation of other people, helping lead you to a better understanding of other people's actions, intentions, and emotions. When you see someone smiling, your mirror neurons for smiling fire up, initiating a cascade of neural activity that evokes the feelings we typically associate with a smile. It doesn't take a conscious effort to experience what the smiler feels because you immediately and effortlessly feel it too.

Remember, the Past Is Not a Prison

The marines have a saying, "Fall down seven times, get up eight." This mantra could easily apply to anyone with effective failure coping mecha-

Don't Give Up

When you find yourself staring misfortune in the face, do what it takes to get up one more time. Don't be a prisoner to past experience. Thomas Edison said, "Many of life's failures are men who did not realize how close they were to success when they gave up."

nisms. Meili, for instance, described to us the first time she went jogging after the Central Park attack. A couple of weeks after she had graduated from using a wheelchair, Nelson, the head of the physical therapy department at her rehab hospital, asked her to join a running group for disabled people who met on the weekends.

> I remember we started out on that hot, humid Saturday morning at what was probably not much faster than a walk. The "track" was a quarter-mile loop through the hospital parking lot and so we came to the end of this little loop and there was a tiny bit of a hill, no more than an upward slope really, but to me it looked like Mount Everest and I started to get a little unsteady. Nelson grabbed a hold of me and we finished the course. If I had it on videotape I'd probably die of embarrassment, but it felt so good! I felt like I had conquered the world.

Obviously she was a far cry from her former accomplished athletic self, but Meili had a strong sense of what she could do in that moment. She realized the attack and subsequent limitations didn't have to define her future. She did what she could to get back in the game without getting hung up on what she could no longer do.

Find a Silver Lining

In October 1945, Andrew Wyeth's father and three-year-old nephew were killed when their car stalled on railroad tracks near their home and was struck by a train. Wyeth, widely considered one of the great American artists of our time, was exceptionally close to his father, N. C. Wyeth, who was one of the great American illustrators of *his* time. "His death really shook me," the artist recalled vividly. "It was a turning point in my career." We interviewed Wyeth at age 91, shortly before his death; it was one of his last interviews, and we are honored to have spoken with someone with such a thoroughly experienced Winner's Brain.

Wyeth felt he had to prove that what his father had taught him really meant something to him so he told us that he began to pull out all the stops: "It gave me a real reason to paint, not just paint pretty scenes, but the emotional core of the way I felt about the loss of him and my loneliness. . . . It wasn't something technical anymore, it became an emotion-

Reframe a failure to find the benefit, even if it's just a tiny nugget. As we learned in the Emotional Balance chapter, Sarah Banks and colleagues have provided fMRI evidence that this act of consciously putting a positive spin on things actually changes brain activity patterns, specifically by engaging areas of the prefrontal cortex, which in turn dampens the response from the amygdalae. Consummate reframers like Wyeth and Meili seem able to tame their amygdalae, and thus negative thoughts, in order to translate even the most difficult circumstances into an affirmative challenge. It's a true Winner's Brain skill. And you won't even need a brain scan to prove how well it works.

ally powerful thing." If you study Wyeth's work done before and after his father's death, you will notice a distinct transition in his painting style.

A tragedy such as the death of a loved one is obviously a setback. It's something that can stop you in your tracks and prevent you from going forward. There is no way to diminish the significance of such an event, but what Wyeth did with his heartbreak is remarkable and a lesson for us all. He found the silver lining in a very dark cloud and instead of becoming paralyzed by his grief, he moved past it in a productive, powerfully positive manner.

When All Else Fails, Take a Break

Have you ever struggled with a problem for a long time only to go for a walk and have the solution suddenly pop into your head? As any scientist, mathematician, or anyone else who wrestles with complex issues on a daily basis will tell you, Eureka moments born from incubating an idea are a very real phenomenon.

A 2008 study by the University of Toronto's Chen-Bo Zhong and his colleagues found that doing something habitual, such as going for a walk, washing the dishes, or taking a nap, enables you to unconsciously access peripheral information your brain may not readily consider during an intense state of Focus. It tends to work better for finding a solution to complex problems like the best seating arrangement for bickering relatives at your wedding or a convoluted financial situation than for straightforward problems such as where to eat dinner or what color shirt to wear. And we speculate that watching TV may be too mind-numbing an activity to best allow the "aha!" to pop out of your brain.

Shifting your attention for a moment can also boost your Resilience because it seems to actively get your brain busy doing something else besides preparing for disaster. Research by scientists in Winnipeg, Canada, has shown, for example, that even the experience of pain can be reduced, along with activity in pain-related regions of the anterior cingulate cortex, by focusing on another task or by actively thinking about something other than the source of pain. Next time you're in a tough situation, try focusing on things like the feel of the chair against your legs, the rumbling of your stomach, or the air as it rushes in and out of your nostrils. The competitive nature of neural activity within the brain region causes a constrained Focus: There simply aren't enough resources to go round, so in effect you can knock the doom-and-gloom processes out of action long enough to focus on something else besides failure.

Whoopi Goldberg may be the poster child for Resilience, but as this chapter demonstrates, everyone can benefit from enhancing this Win Factor. A Winner's Brain is configured to learn from failures—and who doesn't have setbacks?—and take such challenges in stride, reframing them wherever possible as opportunities in disguise. Above all else, you are not defined by your failures. Finding the good, even in the bad, can lead you to the resilient life of a Winner. In the next chapter, we tell you about how the brain's amazing ability to adapt provides the opportunity to shape your grey matter into a Winner's Brain.

Adaptability

Reshaping Your Brain
to Achieve

ADAPTABILITY

The Winner's ability to adapt to changing circumstances is a defining feature of the brain itself. Your brain is always changing. Winners are strategic in taking advantage of this fact, fine-tuning their brain for continued success.

Boost Your BrainPower: All of your BrainPower Tools can be transformed and improved due to the process of neuroplasticity.

IN 2007, SPENCER KELLY, a journalist working for the British Broad-casting Corporation's Web site and television show *Click,* challenged one of London's elite Black Cab drivers to a race through the city against a car equipped with a GPS. A GPS system pulls signals from satellites orbiting the Earth to pinpoint exactly where you are on the planet and then gives you directions to wherever you want to go. The cabbie was equipped with only his humble human brain—which, by now, you know a little something about.

The race started out with Kelly and his GPS in the lead, passing the first checkpoint five minutes ahead of the cabbie. But when the route hit the complex maze of central London, it was all over for the GPS. Despite high-tech traffic avoidance features, the route it chose was choked with congestion and riddled with stops. Meanwhile, the cab zipped down empty side streets, deftly skirting lights and circumventing traffic. By the time the GPS made it to the final checkpoint—27 minutes behind the taxi—the cabbie was already finishing up his tea.

London taxi drivers start out with the same basic brain as anyone else, but, as we learned when we spoke to several of them, they train very hard to gain a near-photographic memory of London, which they reverently refer to as "The Knowledge." "You can't just be good at driving around," one driver named Simon told us in his colorful cockney accent as we sat down over a grilled cheese sandwich in one of 13 cab shelters located in and around the city. "You also have to be good at getting information in your head and keeping it there."

The Knowledge Boys, as cabbies-in-training are known, putter around London on motor scooters for three-plus years with large laminated maps that detail every nook and cranny of the city's sprawling, chockablock six-mile radius mounted to their bug shields. To earn their badge, they must pass an oral and a driving test, both of which cover over 25,000 different streets, 400 different routes or "runs," and thousands of places of interest including hotels, hospitals, statues, theaters, parks, and cemeteries.

"We divide our maps up into grids and once we memorize the basics of a grid, we learn more and more about more and more . . . not only the street names but also which houses have doorbells, where the handicapped ramps are, which lanes will get you there the fastest, that sort of thing," Andy, another cabbie, told us.

Essentially, they use every memory trick in the book, relying heavily on association, repetition, and what Andy calls crossover information, where drivers sit around in their cafes sharing insider tips, like bumblebees transferring pollen between one another in a beehive dance. These cabbies certainly illustrate the Win Factor of Memory. But even more so, they are a perfect example of the seventh factor: Adaptibility. In the process of packing all of this information into their memories, they actually reshape parts of their brains.

When scientists led by Professor Eleanor Maguire at University College London scanned the brains of 16 Black Cab drivers, they discovered that their right hippocampi were appreciably larger than the average person's, particularly in the posterior, or back, of the structures. (The hippocampus, part of the medial temporal lobe, plays a significant role in memory and spatial navigation. It is so named because its curved shape reminded early anatomists of a seahorse; in Greek, hippos means horse, kampos means sea monster.) Furthermore, the more time a driver had spent on the job, the larger his hippocampus grew. The 25-year vets' hippocampi were considerably more developed than the newbies'.

GPS continues to improve, and perhaps someday it will take its tea before the cabbie arrives. But as the London drivers prove, current technology isn't yet as nimble as the highly adaptable, marvelously flexible human brain. The ability to adapt its way of operating—and in some instances, reshape its physical landscape—is a trait known as plasticity, and it's one of the brain's most remarkable characteristics. Neuroscientists believe neuroplasticity is the biological acknowledgment that the world is not constant. We say that it is quite literally the secret to molding a Winner's Brain and the backbone of brainstorm tips in this book.

Adaptability in Action

Early on in this book, we introduced you to Stephen Harris. He's been a world-famous rock star, a successful painter, a rock climbing instructor, and now a medical student on full scholarship at a top medical school. Talk about Adaptability!

"When I decide to do something, I set a goal and in my own quiet way I just decide it's gonna happen," he told us.

Harris, who is from a small seaside town in Wales, is one of those people who is persistently evolving. Like many Winners, he has often changed gears when things were going well for him simply because he felt it was time. That's not to say he's flakey. Becoming the bass player of The Cult at the age of 17—one of the most successful rock bands of the late eighties—took innate talent, yes, but more importantly, thousands of hours practicing guitar in his parents' basement, maintaining a singular Focus on his goal. "My friends would be out doing all sorts of things, but I was on a mission," he says with a laugh. "I could not be deterred."

Harris's decision to become a doctor at the age of 36 came while he was living in New York. He had chosen to leave music behind and was already making a pretty good living as a painter and climbing instructor, but after experiencing the aftermath of the 2001 terrorist attacks on the World Trade Center firsthand, he realized his true calling was medicine. "I was starting with little more than a high school education, which I barely paid attention to," he admits. "I knew art and music, not biochemistry and math, so I was facing thousands of hours of study before I could even apply to medical school—but I just didn't care because it was what I wanted to do."

Though he has never volunteered for an fMRI, we don't need a scan to convince us that Harris's brain has probably adapted in several ways, just as the cabbies' brains changed as a result of their training. That's because the adjustments he made in his actions, goals, and life are signs of his neuroflexibility.

The thing is, the brain keeps on changing no matter what. Moreover, many of these changes depend on what we do with our brain. If you sit around and mope because something doesn't go your way, this mindset may have an ongoing effect on your brain's activity. If you continue to brood day after day, these patterns can lead to ingrained changes in the neural structures themselves. (Indeed, long-term stress and depression can cause areas of the brain to shrink, particularly the hippocampus.) Just as repeatedly engaging in negative thoughts and actions can lead to undesirable brain alterations, actively engaging in more positive thoughts and actions can lead to beneficial ones. Thus, you can take control of your brain and overhaul your life, just as Harris has done several times over. This is only possible through deliberate work, as we will describe later in the chapter.

Here is what really sets Winner's Brains like Harris's apart: They are willing to do the work. They take control over plasticity by intentionally making the changes they want and they deliberately take the steps to think and act in ways that fine-tune their brains and help to achieve their goals. They may make hard work look easy as they fluidly respond to changes taking place around them, but really, they are like ducks on the water: calm on the surface, paddling furiously underneath.

THE MATH AND MUSIC CONNECTION

Perhaps Harris's switch from art to science is not so strange after all. Brain scans taken in 2007 by Vanessa Sluming and other British researchers showed that professional musicians have very busy Broca's areas, a tiny section of the frontal lobe of the cortex that contributes to language production and comprehension. Musical training and regular practice seems to alter brain circuit organization, which, in turn, enhances overall brain power. Conversely, in a recent Turkish study led by Kubilay Aydin, mathematicians who spent the most time working through problems showed increased cortical density in regions of their parietal lobe. The math geeks not only got better at math, they got more creative and better at interpreting 3D objects. The benefit of such carry-over effects is clear: Challenging your brain with all sorts of mental gymnastics can build up your brain muscles the same way a daily walk firms up your body.

What Plasticity Is Made Of

Experts used to think that once you left childhood behind, the brain became more or less a fixed entity and that the different areas of the brain locked themselves into defined roles, unable to be recruited for any other purpose. As Harris's switch from art to medicine demonstrates, the brain remains pliable throughout a lifetime. This is not to say some aspects of the brain don't lose their flexibility as you age, but some jobs can be rerouted and abilities can be maintained. For instance, Ulrika Raue and colleagues at Ball State University reported in 2009 that when they put octogenarian women on a three-month weight training program, they found the women weren't able to increase muscle size or tone the same way younger women can, but even so their leg strength increased by a respectable 26 percent. The researchers concluded the extra power came from how efficiently the women's brains and the nervous systems were able to activate and synchronize their muscles; in effect, their brains reshaped themselves to pick up some of the slack left by waning muscular strength.

Every time you think a thought, feel an emotion, or execute a behavior, there is always some sort of corresponding change to your neurocircuitry. Certainly not every alteration can be detected on an MRI scan, because not all involve enough localized neurons over a long enough period of time. But even a fleeting release of neurotransmitters or a temporary change in electrical activity results in some sort of plasticity. As Bryan Kolb, professor of neuroscience at the University of Lethbridge in Canada, pointed out when we spoke with him, "Some neuroplastic changes happen in a matter of milliseconds, but in and of themselves they aren't likely to make a lasting contribution. Deeply plastic changes can take years."

Even minuscule physical changes can bring about substantial changes in thought and behavior. Indeed, most of the neuropliable changes that take place in adulthood, even those examined in brain studies, are relatively small or might not show up on a scan because they are widely distributed throughout the brain, making them difficult to measure. The resolution of the most advanced MRI scan is not yet powerful enough to detect several million new neural connections if they have formed throughout different parts of the brain.

So what exactly is the stuff of plasticity? On a chemical level, the brain releases a variety of neurotransmitters into synapses, the connections between brain cells. Neurotransmitters are designed to respond in different ways to different situations and environments. When you sit on a park bench relaxing, different nuclei within the brainstem may turn down the dial on norepinephrine (the neurotransmitter that helps keep you alert and aroused) and reward you with a shot of serotonin, a feel-good neurotransmitter. The result is a calmer, happier mood. Conversely, if you sit on the bench worrying about the million things that could go wrong with your day, those feel-good changes will be thwarted by your adrenal glands releasing a shot of cortisol to pump up your anxiety level.

These chemical changes are relatively transient, as are the electrical impulses associated with them, but over time if the signals travel along the same neural pathways often enough, the network of branches and bridges between synapses grows denser and more complex, and in some instances, new neurons form too. All of this new "grey matter" requires energy, so it recruits comparatively large support and maintenance cells known as glia. If your brain generates enough of these support cells, the combined boost in mass shows up on MRI as changes in thickness, volume, and/or density. Interestingly, when neuroscientists report changes in cortical size in MRI studies, they often aren't just talking about the working neurons; they are seeing all of the support cells and infrastructure needed to keep them operational as well.

Now let's examine two schools of thought that prove the power of neuroflexibility.

Mindful Matters

As we wrote in the Self-Awareness chapter, increased self-knowledge endows a Winner's Brain with the interpersonal clarity needed to understand and empathize with the feelings of others. And as we wrote in the Emotional Balance chapter, Winner's Brains are quite skilled at monitoring their own thoughts and feelings, then managing their emotions accordingly. Not surprisingly, these positive changes in attitude and action

Mind Bending

How much meditation or yoga does it take to bring about measurable changes to the brain? Lazar says that there are no good systematic reviews to pin down an exact amount, but she believes most people will derive benefit from doing some sort of meditative practice for just a few minutes a day and adding a more formal practice once a week. "If your mind is racing all the time, even spending some time being aware of your breath or simply counting out ten slow breaths will help calm your thoughts," she says. "In effect you are monitoring your thinking and emotional reactions, which brings about better Emotional Balance as well as measurable brain changes."

are accompanied by changes to the brain. Very few people have more insight into this than Harvard Medical School neuroscientist and psychologist Sara Lazar.

Lazar took up yoga and meditation in her twenties because she got injured training for the Boston Marathon and wanted to do something to improve her flexibility (the bane of nearly anyone who has ever laced up a running shoe). She started taking yoga classes and within a month or so began noticing effects that went well beyond her newfound ability to touch her toes. "It definitely affected my mood and the way I interacted with people—and even with how I viewed life," she recalls.

Her scientific curiosity got the best of her, and she began to wonder if the changes to her well-being were long-lasting. The positive, in-the-moment effects of the meditative state such as the slowing of breath, heart rate, and brain waves were well documented, but Lazar had an inkling that there might be some carryover effect beyond the time she spent with her eyes closed sitting on a cushion. She wanted to know if this effect di-

Lazar also suggests trying to become more aware of what's going on in your mind so you can get some distance from your thoughts. "If you imagine your thoughts flowing by like water in a stream, you can detach from them and focus on the emotional tone behind them. You'll start to see the patterns of emotions and actions. Recognizing those patterns is the first step to changing them."

rectly translated into physical brain changes. In her subsequent years of study, she has found that the answer is yes.

Lazar's various research studies show regular yoga and meditation practice increases cortical thickness in as little as eight weeks. Because the cerebral cortex is comprised of columns of specialized brain cells that form the functional circuits that support cognitive processes, increases in cortical thickness are thought to reflect changes in the density and arrangement of cells in this regard. With meditation, the areas particularly affected include the hippocampus, which matched up with personal reports of decreased stress; parts of the insular cortex involved in sensory awareness, which also makes sense since many types of meditation are focused on improving this trait; and parts of the prefrontal cortex associated with, among other things, attentional control and self-judgment.

Her most recent study showed that just a few short weeks of experience with meditation was enough to already detect increased thickness in the brainstem nuclei responsible for the release of norepinepherine and serotonin, which she was able to correlate with the study volunteer's reports of increased feelings of happiness, well-being, and composure. "I believe that increased serotonin is one big reason why yoga has such a profound effect on quality of life for so many people," she notes.

This takes practice, especially if you don't augment it with formal training, but Lazar says these are accessible skills for just about anyone if rehearsed consistently. "Despite no hard data, I believe a more structured practice will probably produce bigger effects, but taking even just a few mindful minutes a day will have carryover into the rest of your life and result in changes to the brain," she says.

Better Brain Behavior

There are many ways to experience neuroflexibility. In this chapter we met the London cabbies and Stephen Harris, highly determined and self-aware Winners who have managed to reshape their brains through determination and hard work. Yoga and meditation devotees like Lazar have changed their brains using techniques that promote mindfulness and well-being. In fact, all of the people we interviewed for this book have made efforts that rewire their brains, whether they realize it or not.

Some people choose to change their brains (and subsequently their lives) with an approach based on cognitive behavioral psychology. Jeff offers this practical, yet challenging, and effective approach with his clients in the form of cognitive behavioral therapy (CBT). CBT is based on the idea that your thoughts and beliefs affect your feelings and subsequent behaviors. What you believe about yourself, others, and the world around you can directly affect what emotions you feel and how you act. The benefit of this fact? You can change the way you think to feel better and behave differently so you can become more successful in many domains, even if the life circumstances you are trying to overcome remain relatively the same.

On the surface CBT seems simple enough: With the guidance of a licensed clinician, you start by evaluating your strengths and weaknesses and identifying specific, measurable goals. Then, you make an intentional, conscious decision to improve your life by relentlessly committing to making changes in thinking and behaviors so that you ameliorate limitations and play up your strengths.

Just understanding how cognitive behavioral psychology works isn't enough. The new cognitive-behavioral skills must be implemented and practiced routinely. In most cases it takes weeks or months to experience positive change. For some, however, years of hard work may be necessary to break rigid thought patterns and retrain the brain. Regardless, patients who commit to it find that CBT offers a variety of valuable tools for bringing about positive brain changes.

Jeff's patient Mia Wong is an excellent example of someone who used CBT to improve her life. As a second-generation Asian-American, she grew up studying art and dreamed of one day owning her own studio. When Wong went to see Jeff, she already had a good handle on her strengths and weaknesses: She was good at her craft and she dealt with criticism well, but she didn't believe that her work possessed monetary value and didn't feel confident she would be able to earn a living as an artist.

With Jeff's help, Wong began to consider the risks involved in trying to make her art more commercial. She corrected inaccurate beliefs about herself and the value of her work. She became intent about wanting to change and focused on the things she needed to do to move toward her goals. For example, she read all she could get her hands on about artists and business, art communities, and other art forms and she joined a local artists' cooperative so she could speak to already successful artists about how best to present her work and avoid pitfalls. To boost her confidence, she began rehearsing thoughts like "My work competes with other successful artists in the cooperative" and "Collectors buy my art by choice."

After a while, she noticed her lack of self-confidence had disappeared. She was changing how she thought about herself and her profession and was deliberately rethinking factors in her life so she could find evidence to believe the best of herself and work. And of course, as a Winner, Wong didn't stop there. As her career and success grew, she continued to reinforce the strategies that helped her make the transformation, and she continued to find joy in her work and her life by redirecting her thoughts and energy in the direction of her professional goals. In the end, the cognitive restructuring of her thoughts effectively rearranged her neurocircuitry for the better.

If you have never experienced CBT, Wong's story may sound more like luck than plasticity, but there is plenty of science behind it. One of the best examples of this is a recent study led by Greg Siegle in Pittsburg which found that CBT calmed the amygdala response in patients prone to emotional overreaction—and it did so more effectively than antidepressant medication. Furthermore, the effects of CBT lasted even after therapy ended, while the effects of the medication wore off shortly after the subjects stopped taking it. The end result of this change in brain activity was improved Emotional Balance over the long term for CBT participants compared to those who took medication or the control group.

Kolb's comments to us resonate with these findings: "CBT should be viewed as invasive, because any change in behavior must be reflected in brain change. When you train people in a new way of thinking, by definition, it involves different neural networks."

That said, Kolb cautions that because CBT takes time to redirect thoughts, and by extension, make alterations to the brain, it won't work until those changes are in place. "Sometimes people will argue that it's not working," he says. "But you have to ask, 'How long did it take you to get to the state you are in, in the first place?' It may take at least that long to see the changes because you have to recruit whole new networks involved in coping strategies and overcome automatic routines."

Many tips we have given throughout this book are fast and easy to implement, and some of them are even inspired by common CBT practices. CBT is no quick fix, but it can make real, important differences in your life. And, as straightforward as the tenets of CBT seem, they are most successful when you work through them with an experienced and qualified clinician. If you are really serious about banishing negative thought patterns and encouraging positive ones to reshape your brain and to reorient your life in a better direction, CBT is an effective game plan.

The Three Faces of Hope

It's tempting to think of plasticity as something that happens when you change a behavior because those things often translate directly into a new skill such as learning to swing a golf club or mastering a new software program. But the fact is, you often experience neuroflexibility through emotion. The following CBT exercise called "The Three Faces of Hope" illustrates this perfectly.

On a scale of 1 to 10 with 1 being none and 10 being the most, rate how hopeful you feel about your life so far and your future to come.

Next, choose three important, positive people in your life—someone from the past, someone from the present, and someone you wish to meet in the future. Visualize each person, one at a time, imagining why each of these individuals would want you to feel hope. Use all of your senses and let your brain fully imagine the experience of being with that person; see their smiles, hear their words of support, feel the warmth of their encouragement.

Now, using that same scale, has the strength of your hope changed? If it has, not only have you successfully changed your brain, you've measured that change in a meaningful way. Don't be surprised if the strength of your feeling of hope moves around. If you practice this sort of thought-changing exercise often enough, your brain may adapt so that hope becomes a more prominent emotion.

SPOTTING PLASTICITY

Here's a quick exercise to demonstrate plasticity in action. Look at the picture below. Do you see the dalmatian? Stare at it long enough and you will. As the visual signals travel from your retina through to your visual cortex, the shape of the dog in the image resonates with similar representations in memory stored in areas of the temporal lobe so that you are able to organize what you see into an interpretable shape. If Mark, our resident neuroscientist, were to scan your brain both before and after you were able to bring the dog into focus, he would be hard-pressed to pinpoint any definable, physical differences. Yet clearly there is some sort of neuroflexibility going on here, because the change itself is typically permanent: Once you can see the dog, you should be able to see it from now on.

R. L. Gregory, *The Intelligent Eye* (1970). London: Weidenfeld and Nicholson.

Back to Basics

In various other chapters we have mentioned that practicing something diligently until it is on automatic pilot can improve everything from Focus to Memory to Emotional Balance. However, if you are really struggling with something you are normally good at, Kolb advises revisiting the fundamentals. "When your brain performs something that is completely automatic you can sometimes lose many of the finer points of the skill," he explains.

Studies done on professional musicians show that some practice to such an extent that they lose the ability to use their fingers independently, a condition known as focal hand dystonia. This seems to be a case of neuroplasticity gone awry. In its bid to increase efficiency, their brains processed the neural activity associated with the fine-grained, repetitive finger movements involved in playing their instruments and responded by blending together areas of the sensory-motor cortex that were originally mapped out independently for each different finger. Without distinct regions of the cortex assigned to each finger, they lose the ability to move them independently from one another. In this case a remedy reported by German researcher Victor Candia and his colleagues was to have the musicians wear a splint to hold unnecessary fingers still until the cortical areas were remapped back to their original state.

So if you find yourself in a slump with something you're normally good at, try a reboot. Take a few lessons, read a book geared toward beginners, or practice some basic drills. Top athletes we've spoken with do this frequently, but it also applies to just about any skill or task where you find yourself stuck in a rut. "In some cases," says Kolb, "becoming more conscious by breaking things down step by step can actually help tune up your system."

The brain has an amazing power to reshape itself, even well into old age. Winners take control over their brain's Adaptability. Certain techniques such as meditation, yoga, and cognitive behavioral psychology are proven to have positive effects on how the brain adapts. Just as all the BrainPower Tools or Win Factors depend upon the power of this neuroflexibility, they also rely on how you care for your brain, the subject of our next and final chapter.

Brain Care

Maintaining, Protecting,
and Enhancing
Your Winner's Brain

BRAIN CARE

Your brain, much like the rest of your body, has fundamental needs. By doing plenty of physical activity, providing your brain with rich and meaningful experiences, sleeping well, and eating a proper diet, you can help meet these needs and help give yourself the edge it takes to cultivate a Winner's Brain.

Boost Your BrainPower: Care and feeding of the brain is another thing that enhances all BrainPower Tools. Much like your car, your brain runs better on premium fuel and regular tune-ups.

OPTIMAL BRAIN FUNCTION is not a case of nature trumping nurture. It's also how you nurture what nature gave you. It's true that your genetic material provides a set of blueprints that outline the potential structure and function of your brain. But, however well-designed those blueprints are, you can only fully realize your brain's capabilities and optimize them when you treat your brain right.

Just as there are necessary habits for the proper maintenance of a high-performance body, so too are there necessary habits for maintaining a high-performance brain. And it turns out that what is good for the body is usually good for the brain (which is after all part of the body). We've identified four brain-care habits that are of particular importance for a healthy brain: physical activity, providing your brain with rich and meaningful experiences, eating a brain-healthy diet, and getting plenty of good sleep. Let's take a moment to talk about why each of these is so helpful in building, protecting, and maintaining a Winner's Brain.

Success on the Run

Almost everyone would agree with the assumption that exercise will help a child lose weight and get healthy. But would they necessarily expect that child to also improve his ability to remember? To focus? To become more motivated and emotionally balanced? This is what middle-school teacher Allison Cameron wondered as she considered ways to get her City Park Collegiate students to better concentrate on their schoolwork. City Park Collegiate is an inner-city school that specializes in helping kids with learning issues and personal problems in Saskatoon, the largest city in the Canadian province of Saskatchewan. To test this idea, over a period of four months, Cameron had her students pedal stationary bikes and run on treadmills during language arts class. For math class, they headed off to the weight room and pumped iron while pondering the day's arithmetic problems.

Those exercise sessions every other day over the course of a semester translated into academic rewards beyond her expectations. "To my amazement, every single student went up at least one full grade in reading and writing and some kids went up six full grades in their vocabulary scores," Cameron says.

By the end of the four-month trial, the students' ability to concentrate was sharper and they spent more time working without interruption. Attendance also improved and disciplinary problems nosedived by 67 percent. There was even a decrease in the use of medications, such as Ritalin, used to treat concentration-related impairments. None of these results should really be too surprising: Exercise has such a positive, generalized effect on your brain, it almost makes the benefits to the heart, lungs, and muscles seem incidental. Recent neuroimaging and cognitive psychological studies, such as those reviewed in 2009 by Christopher Hertzog and colleagues, have documented how a regular exercise program can increase attentional focus, improve learning and memory, reduce impulsivity, enhance mood, lower stress, and increase the volume of important structures in the brain. These findings appear to be true whether you are a high school student who jogs during class or a golden ager who takes a daily stroll.

At the most basic level, exercise brings oxygen and glucose into the brain. Think of glucose as the brain's main fuel source and oxygen as the means of ignition. During a session of cardiovascular exercise, such as running, swimming, or cycling, blood circulation speeds up and the lungs soak up a higher volume of oxygen from the air. The result is a more generous slug of oxygen to the brain, which enables neurons to release the energy stored in high-energy chemical bonds within the glucose in the food we eat, and enables them to use that energy to do what neurons do: namely, keep the brain firing. This turns the brain into a star performer—a Winner's Brain.

Regular workouts can increase the capacity of capillaries serving the brain so there is better blood flow and oxygen uptake all of the time, not just when you're working up a sweat. Increased blood volume is good for the brain in other ways too. It promotes the growth of new neural connections and support cells as well as the delivery of an assortment of beneficial molecules, including brain-derived neurotrophic factors (BDNFs). Ongoing studies such as that led by Heather Oliff at the University of California, Irvine, identified the numerous brain-building advantages of elevated BDNFs, including the ability to promote change in the hippocampus, an area of the brain critically involved in memory and learning. The main link between exercise, BDNFs, and the hippocampus involves both synaptic plasticity, the growth and strengthening of connections between neurons, and neurogenesis, the growth of brand-new neurons. Exercise is one of the few things that can actually result in the adult brain growing new neurons, not just new synaptic connections.

Exercise is especially useful for helping your brain stay in good working order as you age. According to Arthur Kramer, professor of psychology at the University of Illinois at Urbana-Champaign, being physically active can actively slow age-related shrinkage of the prefrontal cortex, which is important for preserving executive-type functions. Executive functions are a relatively broad set of cognitive abilities that include, to name a few, your ability to plan, problem solve, and manage attention. You'll recognize the direct influence exercise has on the Winner's Brain

Strengthening Your Mind

Kramer's own body of research suggests that 30 minutes of moderate physical activity, three times a week, works pretty well for boosting and preserving brain power. And, he speculates, there is not yet enough evidence to show that pushing yourself harder or taking up marathoning bestows significantly greater advantages.

He is also quick to point out that there are many ways to stay active. "Keep in mind that all physical activity helps maintain mental faculties, not just formal exercise," he comments. "Moving on a regular basis can push the clock back two to three years with regard to cognition, both broad and specific." So every time you tend your garden, stack a cord of wood, play tag with your kids, or mop the floor, you're helping to age-proof your brain.

in such areas as Self-Awareness, Focus, and Emotional Balance. According to Kramer, "Executive function starts to decline when people reach their 70s, but lifelong exercisers preserve executive function much better than sedentary people do."

Kramer says people who begin exercising in middle age significantly reduce their risk of dementia and are less likely to suffer from Alzheimer's disease. Also, by improving cardiovascular health, exercise prevents heart attacks and strokes, which often cause brain damage. Even non-movers who don't manage to rise up off the couch until later in life can still lower their risk of cognitive decline. Eric Larson and his team of Seattle-based researchers recently determined, for instance, that seniors who exercised at least three times a week diminished their risk of dementia by up to 32 percent.

In 2009, Kramer and his colleagues at the University of Illinois and the University of Pittsburgh published a study that found elderly adults who were physically fit tended to have bigger hippocampi and better spatial memory than those who were less fit. Amazingly, the study linked hippocampus size in the fitter subjects to 40 percent of their advantage in spatial memory. But that does not mean you need to dedicate your life to the gym to see all of these amazing benefits.

Inspire Your Brain

While exercise seems to offer the brain across-the-board cognitive advantages, you can stimulate your mind in other ways that zero in on specific brain functions. You may remember from the Focus chapter, for instance, that video games can improve the ability to control the focus of attention; or, from the Memory chapter, how taking the time to create an associative picture of an object in your mind will create a deeper imprint of that object in your memory. While playing a video game or learning to memorize grocery lists helps you get better at gaming and loading your grocery cart, such mental exercises may also have some important carry-over effects for other tasks that rely on the same cognitive processes or underlying neural structures. The effects that follow from such mental stimulation reflect the neuroplastic changes within the brain itself.

Consider what happens to rat pups when a researcher comes by every few hours and gently brushes their fur with a soft paint brush. While it may seem like an odd thing to do, simply rubbing, brushing, or even blowing on a rat pup's skin enhances their neural development by stimulating the release of a brain chemical known as fibroblast growth factor-2 (FGF2). In 2009, Javier Perez and a team of researchers at the University of Michigan reported that the release of FGF2 as a result of brushing their rodent subjects seemed to help reduce the rats' anxiety and improve their memory. The researchers found that high-anxiety rats produced the same number of new brain cells in the hippocampus as low-anxiety rats, but the furry worriers had fewer surviving new brain cells than their more carefree cage mates. (Though it does make one wonder what a lab rat worries about.)

We humans also benefit from what scientists call "an enriched environment." To a lab rat, an enriched environment means getting stroked with a paint brush, or nibbling on a variety of foods, and living in a colorful cage filled with lots of squeaky toys. To us humans, it means living an interesting life full of challenges, relationships, and accomplishments. "The effects of environmental factors on neuroplasticity are so complex," notes Bryan Kolb, "the experiences your mother had while you were in the womb and even experiences she herself had as a child can have an effect on how your brain works."

In childhood, when your brain is busy establishing fresh neural connections, it is like a sponge, soaking up new memories, skills, and abilities with comparative ease. An inevitable consequence of aging is that your cognitive potential tends to diminish. But as we explained in the Adaptability chapter, your brain retains much of its ability to reshape and reinvent itself until the day you die. There are limitless opportunities for stimulating your brain throughout your lifetime.

Even something as basic as enjoying a hobby has been shown to delay or prevent memory loss. A 2009 study by Yonas Geda and other researchers at the Mayo Clinic found that seniors as old as 89 who kept busy with hobbies like quilting, reading books, playing board games, or surfing the Web lowered their risk of memory loss by 30 to 50 percent compared to people who pursued no hobbies. (In the same study, those who watched television for more than seven hours a day were 50 percent more likely to develop memory loss.)

A recent study conducted by Gary Small and researchers at the University of California, Los Angeles involved 24 middle-aged and older subjects with normally functioning brains. It came to a similar conclusion regarding another simple pastime: When the participants performed search tasks on the Internet, fMRI scans detected a flurry of activity throughout much of the brain, including regions often associated with controlling language, reading, memory, and visual abilities. Furthermore, the amount of activation in these regions was much greater for individuals with previous online-searching experience than for those who were Net novices, suggesting that the more they surfed, the more engaged their neural networks became.

Food for Thought

If you decide to browse the Web as a way of expanding your mind, surf on over to your favorite bookseller's site and type the word "diet" into the search function. You'll get hits for nearly 400,000 titles. In this diet-obsessed society, it seems the experts can't agree whether we should be eating like cavemen or nibbling like rabbits. From our point of view, what goes past your lips may or may not go directly to your hips—but it always goes to your brain. Regardless of the specific diet plan you follow, a Winner's Brain needs certain, critical ingredients to operate on all cylinders.

Fat is one of those critical ingredients. Putting aside the decades of anti-fat messages for a moment, bear in mind that your brain is nearly 60 percent fat. Along with water, fats are a chief component of brain cell membranes and the myelinated sheath layer that wraps around the axons of neurons to protect and enhance their ability to communicate.

That doesn't mean you rush to the nearest fast food joint and shout, "Super size me!" The kind of fat found in burgers, fries, and ice cream isn't the kind that contains the building blocks for the Winner's Brain. Good "brain fat" is found in foods like fish, walnuts, canola oil, and eggs. These contain polyunsaturated fats derived from long-chain omega-3 fatty acids with eicosapentaenoic acid (EPA) and docosahexaenoic acid (DHA). A second type of good brain fat, known as linoleic acid (LA), is the foundation of the omega-6 family of fatty acids.

Brain Food

Experts recommend a 4:1 omega-6-to-omega-3 ratio for optimal brain function. One way to achieve this balance is to eat a few servings a week of cold water fish such as salmon and mackerel or foods fortified with fatty acids. Plant sources such as seeds and nuts are useful but more difficult for the body to break down and process.

You get this type of fat in your diet from vegetable oils, nuts, and seeds. Together, omega-3 and -6 are referred to as the essential fats, so named because it is important that you include them in your diet.

Essential fatty acids (EFAs) are critical for superior brain power because they help determine the fluidity of neuronal membranes and because they are involved in the synthesis and functions of many of the brain's neurotransmitters. Your brain needs a continuous supply of EFAs throughout your life, but recently a team led by Shlomo Yehuda of Bar Ilan University noted that there are two particularly sensitive periods where a deficit can have major implications—infancy and aging. An EFA deficiency in infancy can delay brain development, and in aging, it can accelerate deterioration of brain functions. EFAs have been shown to preserve and enhance memory by blocking the build-up of brain plaque; they also protect against Alzheimer's disease and depression by ensuring a steady supply of neurotransmitters, especially the happiness chemicals, norepinephrine, serotonin, and dopamine.

Beyond providing EFAs, fish truly gets the silver platter for being a Winner's Brain food because it is high in vitamin D. A large British trial published late in 2009 by Alan Dangour and colleagues found that eating fish a few times a week is so good for grey matter that it helped people, especially seniors, perform better on simple memory and attention tasks.

Two Apples a Day

The results obtained from the mice study were comparable to humans drinking approximately two eight-ounce glasses of apple juice, or eating two or three apples daily. In the blueberry study, the subjects ate about half a cup of the tasty little fruits each day. The largest brain gains seem to result from eating fresh fruit and drinking unfiltered juices so most of the phytochemicals, vitamins, and minerals are preserved.

Other sources offer some of these benefits too, though fish seems to be the perfect combination of EFAs and brain-building vitamins. That said, you should always consider mercury levels found in many fish species by checking local fish advisories and general recommendations for safe and environmentally sustainable consumption.

There is also good evidence that many fruits and vegetables enrich memory and learning and may help keep the brain young. In one recent study, Amy Chan and her University of Massachusetts, Lowell colleagues found that adding apples and apple juice to the diet protected genetically deficient mice from both their genetic shortcomings and a poor diet, allowing them to perform at the same level on memory and learning tests as normal mice who dined on a variety of foods. A 2008 investigation conducted in Britain by Claire Williams and other researchers found that a regular diet supplemented with blueberries resulted in significant improvements to spatial working memory in just three weeks with continuous improvement throughout the entire three months the study lasted.

Apples are full of antioxidants that help guard against the oxidative damage to brain cells, and berries, especially blueberries, are bursting with flavinoids which appear to cross the blood-brain barrier to boost synaptic connections and stimulate brain cell regeneration, especially in the hippocampus. Grapes, plums, onions, and many other fruits and vegetables high in antioxidants are also being studied for their ability to turbocharge the brain.

Sleeping Your Way to Success

Diet-obsessed we may be, but one Brain Care strategy many of us neglect is sleep. If we cut back on calories the same way we withhold sleep, we would be a society of anorexics.

Sleep is vital for optimal brain function. Anyone who has ever gone without the full forty winks knows how hard it is to function or think. Doctors, pilots, soldiers, and shift workers are all expected to perform well despite interrupted sleep woven into the fabric of their profession. And what parent of a newborn hasn't packed a travel bag with two left shoes and no diapers after a couple of nights of waking up every two hours?

Philip Calhoun, a 48-year-old natural gas operator, knows this perhaps better than anyone. He is a past winner of the annual *Hand on a Hardbody* competition held at the Joe Mallard Nissan car dealership in Longview, Texas. Each year, 24 contestants attempt to outlast each other by standing in the large asphalt parking lot under the hot September sun with one hand resting on a brand-new Nissan Frontier truck, no leaning or squatting down allowed. The last person to take their hand off the $38,000 vehicle drives it home.

Calhoun entered once before and was disqualified after 90 hours when he couldn't stand back up after the hourly break. It took him five years to work up the Motivation to try again, but as someone equipped with a fierce Goal Laser and a steady Effort Accelerator, he readied himself by working out like a demon, studying up on diet and mental strategies, and employing many of the Winner's Brain strategies we've already mentioned. But in the end, trying to stay awake for so long nearly did him in. As Calhoun notes, "There is really no way to prepare for going nearly four days without sleep."

"At around the eightieth hour I lost my mind. I didn't even know where I was or what I was doing," the strapping Texan recalls.

Looking out at the crowd of 2,000 spectators, seriously sleep-deprived Calhoun was convinced they were clapping, cheering, and waving banners because he was a big Hollywood star in the middle of shooting a movie. Drawing deeply on his powers of Motivation, Focus, and Emotional Balance, Calhoun hung tough. He won after 93 hours when the only other remaining contestant simply lifted her hand off the truck and wandered off in a daze.

Not that average people typically push themselves to the point of hallucinating, but depriving yourself of a decent night's sleep can send the brain into a tailspin. A 2007 fMRI study done by Harvard Medical School researcher Seung-Schik Yoo and his colleagues at the University of California, Berkeley, provided some of the first evidence that poor sleep brings on profound changes in the amygdala. (You'll remember that the amygdala is a small structure in the medial temporal lobe that is often involved in emotion-related processes.) With no sleep, amygdala response to emotional images appears to go into overdrive, disrupting communication with areas of the prefrontal cortex typically associated with logical reasoning and thus preventing feedback signals needed to calm down the fight-or-flight reflex. The result of this may be temporary depression or anxiety. It is almost as though, without sleep, the brain is unable to put emotional experiences into context to produce controlled, appropriate responses.

Thankfully a good night's sleep (or two or three in a row) restores the balance of communication between the prefrontal cortex, the amygdala, and other emotion-related centers, allowing most people to regain a firm hold on the reins of Emotional Balance. In general, brain restoration is one of sleep's main functions, although it's not completely understood *what* is being restored.

One theory is that rapid eye movement (REM) sleep replenishes glycogen, a stored-form of glucose that is the brain's only source of back-up energy. Glycogen supplies are scant (as we've already mentioned, most of the brain's energy comes directly from glucose in the bloodstream), but localized regions of the brain rely on these supplies during highly active periods, much like an appliance drawing upon a spare generator.

A good rest may also provide the brain with a chance to rebuild its cache of neurotransmitters, neural growth factors, and cell-building proteins, which gradually become depleted during waking hours. Brain glycogen loss has been shown to trigger the release of adenosine, a neurotransmitting chemical that appears to decrease wakefulness and induce sleepiness. Chemicals important to the immune system are also secreted by the brain during sleep. Interestingly, experts think that people who "die of sleep deprivation" may actually succumb to illness brought on by a weak immune system rather than lack of sleep.

Sleep seems to be important for consolidating memories, possibly allowing the brain to build stronger interconnectivity between the hippocampus and other areas important for memory storage. One fascinating 2007 study conducted in Liège, Belgium, by Virginie Sterpenich and others found that subjects could recall information they'd learned up to six months later if they'd immediately slept on it for at least six hours than if they had to go without the post-learning snooze. Comparing fMRI scans from these conditions, the researchers concluded that going to sleep after learning something seems to enhance communication between the hippocampus and the medial prefrontal cortex, and they suggest that this helps to transform initially fragile memories into those that are more deeply imprinted. Evidence presented in a recent review of related research also suggests that memory enhancement that occurs during sleep is due to a release of biomolecules that help strengthen synapses and improve the connection between neurons. Other studies such as that by Ullrich Wagner and his German colleagues have shown how REM sleep appears to make the brain better at learning, thinking, and organizing information; this may be why you sometimes drift off thinking about a difficult problem and the solution pops into your head as soon as you wake up.

Whatever the reason, no one disagrees with the notion that sleep can influence all sorts of brain functions, including those related to a Winner's Brain. "It's clear that the people who live the longest and are cognitively still aware into old age have the most intact sleep," notes Carlyle Smith, a distinguished sleep researcher and psychology professor at Trent University in Ontario. He told us that his own research suggests that a full night's rest can translate into a 20 to 30 percent improvement in the performance of motor tasks, such as those involved in sports skills.

Unfortunately for many of us, getting a decent night's rest is, well, just a dream. More than 60 million Americans suffer from insomnia, which Smith says tends to worsen with age, when we begin to skim along the surface of wakefulness for much more of the night than when we are in our twenties. Even with innate talents and a focus on brain-building strategies, a Winner's Brain can't operate properly without enough sleep. Smith's research confirms that this is the seven to eight hours a night typically recommended.

The Power of Meditation

In previous chapters, we've sung the praises of meditation and its power to change the brain for the better. Work done by people like Sara Lazar, a neuroscientist and researcher at Massachusetts General Hospital, show how regular meditation alters the actual structure of the cortex and increases thickness in brain regions associated with attention and sensory

Four Tips for 40 Winks

While Smith says that most of the customary tips for sound sleep are right—setting a regular sleep schedule, relaxing, turning off the TV—he warns against taking the standard advice of having a hot bath before bedtime. "This is likely to backfire because it artificially elevates body temperature and makes it harder to drift off," he comments. "Believe it or not, taking a cool or tepid shower works better because it lowers your body temperature, which is one of the body's signals to drift off."

Keeping a food and sleep journal may help you figure out dietary insomnia triggers. Allergies to foods like chocolate, corn, and aspartame are often the cause of sleep troubles. Another culprit can be late-night meals, which can elevate body temperature.

As for sleeping pills, Smith says most help you mime the physical act of sleep without offering most of the restorative effects, so they won't do much for building a Winner's Brain. Although many drugs do their best not to interfere with REM sleep, the majority actually mangle it. If you really need something to help you drift off and stay asleep, Smith says studies seem to indicate that meditation is one of the best sleep aids around—though with diminishing returns. "People who meditate up to 30 minutes a day will sleep better, but those who meditate for longer have actually been shown to have interrupted sleep, possibly because their brains have gotten something from the meditation that they would normally get while sleeping."

processing. Name any Win Factor strategy and even small daily doses of meditation seem to augment it. Those benefits can be seen during the very first session: When Lazar monitored novice meditator's brains with fMRI scans, she picked up more organized patterns of activity as they sat quietly with their eyes closed, possible signs that the brain was calmer and more focused. In those with more experience, these changes become deeper and seem to appear even when a person is not sitting on the meditation cushion.

If you aren't already convinced that meditation is a worthwhile pursuit, try this: Close your eyes and take ten deep, slow breaths. Even if you do this while standing in the middle of a crowded subway train or sitting at your kid's soccer practice, it will have the immediate effect of sweeping fresh oxygen into your brain so you feel more relaxed and clear minded. And this is just a small taste of what mediation can do for you. Naturally, meditation is more effective when you find a quiet, comfortable place to sit, add a plant, open a window, and take the time to quiet your mind and relax your body.

Do "Neurobics" work?

The budding industry for brain-training products—already worth $125 million a year—banks on the fact that 20 minutes a day of mental gymnastics in the form of a computer game will sharpen memory. Sellers promise their games will reverse ten years of brain aging and mitigate neuro-degenerative diseases after just eight weeks of daily mental workouts.

These games are selling like hotcakes, but so far, there's little evidence to support those claims. To date, no double-blind randomized study on these products exists that has been performed by an unbiased source, so all improvements to things like Memory, Focus, and Attention remain mere speculation.

Stretch Your Brain

For now, anyone looking for a tried and true method of pursuing a Winner's Brain should take up a proven brain-training technique such as learning a new language, playing a musical instrument, or signing up for a math class. Or, they could practice the one brain-building exercise that study after study shows will result in better overall brain fitness: physical activity.

Not that experts are necessarily against trying out these games—they certainly won't hurt—but many speculate that brain gamers may simply get good at playing the games and little more. It could be that once you've got a handle on the game's strategies, your brain is no longer required to stretch any further and there is no general enhancement of cognitive fitness. The same may be true of pastimes like crossword and Sudoku puzzles. There's simply not yet enough proof either way.

Brain Buzz

Are you one of those people who can't seem to roll out of bed without having a cup of coffee first? As long as you don't overdo it, this may not be such a bad thing.

Caffeine perks you up because the brain perceives it as similar to the neurotransmitter adenosine, whose job it is to slow the brain down and lull it into a state of drowsiness. As you sip your morning java, the caffeine binds to adenosine receptors in the basal forebrain so they can no longer latch onto the adenosine. Without the adenosine, the nerve cells speed up instead of slowing down, and thus stop you from feeling tired, at least for a few hours. Caffeine has also been shown to increase production of both adrenaline and dopamine, simultaneously making you feel more alert and happier.

This is all well and good, and, as Carrie Ruxton found in a 2008 meta-analysis, moderate daily caffeine intake—one to four cups—does provide emotional and cognitive advantages such as improved mood, better memory, and alertness for most people. Problems seem to arise only when you pour one cup too many or caffeinate yourself too late in the day; the average cup of brewed coffee contains about 100 milligrams of caffeine, which can delay the urge to sleep by two to three hours.

The average person will start to feel the adverse effects of caffeine with 500 to 600 milligrams in their system, the equivalent of four to seven cups of coffee. You'll know you've had too much if you start to feel over-stimulated, anxious, or dehydrated or your head starts pounding. Beware other sources of caffeine that may unwittingly pump up your caffeine intake to unhealthy levels. Some energy drinks contain nearly double the amount of caffeine found in coffee and some specialty takeout coffees contain nearly triple the usual amount.

This final Win Factor includes the most essential aspects of Brain Care: physical and mental activity, diet, a rich and stimulating environment, and sleep. These are the basics for keeping your brain healthy and functioning optimally. Most of these are simple changes you can make that can have a big impact on how smoothly your brain functions. All of them—especially when combined with the strategies that support the other seven Win Factors—can help prime your mind for success.

Brain Care at a Glance

Exercise	Stimulation	Nutrition	Sleep
Get 30 minutes of formal physical activity at least 3 times a week	Engage in a hobby on a regular basis; this may include quilting, reading, or surfing the Internet	Add half a cup of berries to your daily diet	Aim for 7 to 8 hours of uninterrupted sleep each night
Accumulate additional physical activity of any type for at least 30 minutes, 3 times a week	Emphasize rich and varied experiences that involve as many of the five senses as possible	Aim for a 4:1 ratio of omega-6 to omega-3 free fatty acids; eating fish is the easiest way to pump up omega-3s	Develop a relaxing bedtime ritual

Aim to lower body temperature to induce sleep; take a cool or tepid shower before bedtime rather than a hot bath |
| Commit to a regular exercise program regardless of your previous history and your age | Brain games may not enhance all aspects of cognition but will improve the specific skills used in game play; ditto for crossword puzzles and Sudoku

Meditate or do deep breathing relaxation exercises or yoga for 30 minutes, 3 times per week or more | Drink 2 to 3, 8-ounce glasses of apple juice or eat 2 to 3 apples per day

Consider adding onions, cherries, and plums as well as a variety of other fruits and veggies to your diet

Limit caffeine consumption to the earlier part of the day and ingest no more than 500 to 600 milligrams daily, the equivalent of 6 to 7 cups of coffee | Keep a food and sleep journal to get a handle on food allergies and eating habits that affect sleep

Skip sleep medications |

Epilogue

I N THE WINTER OF 1949, B. B. King was performing at a small club in Twist, Arkansas, when two men got into a fight and knocked over a kerosene stove, setting fire to the hall. King raced outdoors to safety, then realized he had left his beloved $30 acoustic guitar inside, so he rushed back inside the burning building to retrieve it, narrowly escaping death. Two other men weren't as lucky and died in the flames. When King later found out the fight had been over a woman named Lucille, he decided to give the same name to his guitar to remind him never to do something as stupid as fight over a woman—or run into a burning building. Since then, each one of King's trademark Gibson guitars has been called Lucille.

Although this story is not the finest demonstration of Optimal Risk Gauge, the lessons King took away from such a foolish act are good ones. Understanding what's important and not sweating the small stuff takes, among other things, Resilience, Focus, and Emotional Balance. Most people would agree these are traits that personify King's character and career. And these are also the types of abilities we hope you have begun to strengthen by reading *The Winner's Brain*.

The people we interviewed for this book are living proof of the science, which shows that success is defined not by where you are born, how smart you are, or how much money you have—or even by dumb luck. Success is attained by using your brain's faculties to respond to the circumstances and challenges you face in life. B. B. King grew up poor. As he told us, "If I had it to do over again I would prefer not to grow up in a segregated society; I would have gone to college to study computer science and I wouldn't have gotten married until after I was forty. Still, most of the things that happened to me I wouldn't change. Even the hardships—these made me who I am."

As we've said throughout this book, we believe that people who meet their personal definition of "making it" have been able to plow through obstacles and rise to any challenge that stands in the way of achieving their goals. We believe they succeed because they have brains that operate in a very special way to optimize their thoughts, behaviors, and emotions. Although we didn't subject King to a brain scan, his achievements and the studies of other individuals, musicians and non-musicians alike, provide some insight into how his fine-tuned neurocircuitry has served him so well.

In the Motivation chapter, we mentioned the study by Charles Limb and Allen Braun that examined the brains of talented jazz musicians. It revealed that composing-on-the-fly periods of jazz improvisation are accompanied by disengagement of brain regions associated with cognitive monitoring and control, such as the dorsolateral prefrontal cortex, and an enhancement of activity in areas associated with self-expression, such as the medial prefrontal cortex. Such dynamic changes in brain function seem to allow these artists to break free of any creative constraints and simply let the music flow.

B. B. King knows the feeling well: "I seem to be living in the moment where every note is like finding a missing piece to a puzzle. When you find the pieces, it's like a river flowing."

The words "flow" and "flowing" are apt; scientists refer to this phenomenon as "flow state." And, as we explained in the Motivation chapter, you don't have to be an exceptional improvisationalist in order to achieve flow state or to benefit from the heightened sense of creativity and motivation it induces. People from all walks of life, whether they work in marketing, acting, or window washing, describe a similar state of mind when they feel able to effortlessly spin new ideas and creative solutions. If you can train yourself to be consistently and highly motivated—and we hope that you can by using the strategies we have offered—you may learn to let your brain go in this way, and experience the creative surge King describes so beautifully.

Flow is just one of the many amazing things a Winner's Brain can achieve. By now you know that Winners channel the marvelous adaptability and flexibility of the brain to shape it in the directions they want it to go. And even if you've never tried to improve your cognitive strengths, there is nothing stopping you from trying to transform your thinking, emotions, and behavior by optimizing the way your brain operates. Besides Motivation and Adaptability, you now know neurocognitive strategies for greater Self-Awareness, Focus, and Emotional Balance, improved Memory, and stronger Resilience; and you also have the best information available for the care and feeding of your brain. All of these skills will help improve how you use and shape specific areas of your brain, which in turn contribute to a stronger, healthier Winner's Profile.

In 1946, at the age of 21, King left his hometown in Mississippi for Memphis, Tennessee, to live with his cousin Bukka White, a famous guitarist and singer. By then King knew he wanted to spend his life making music and took advantage of the ten months he lived with his cousin to study technique and performance. However, he realized he needed to be better prepared for success so he returned home to work at the local R&B radio station, WDIA, as a singer and disc jockey. He spent two years honing his craft before returning to Memphis, this time armed with more confidence and vastly superior skills. Although his first recordings in 1949 were not well received, he persevered. Known for his incredible work ethic, King never stopped studying, learning, and practicing. Clearly, it paid off. By the 1950s he was already regarded as an important R&B artist.

Now in his eighties and a music legend, King still strives to do better. "Any day I don't hear or learn something new is a day lost. I practice and work on my music because I want to learn," he told us. "I don't think of my age as a shut-off valve. I do everything I can to make sure I have a good night."

This is the crib notes description of King's life and career. But even in the abridged version, his Winner's Brain comes shining through. His Goal Laser and Effort Accelerator have certainly helped propel him from poverty to become the undisputed King of the Blues, and his Talent Meter and Opportunity Radar must have helped him make the right choices along the way. Without the benefit of money or even much formal education or training, he managed to use many of the Win Factor strategies we've outlined in this book.

It's worth noting that, for someone who personifies the sound of soul, it was King's brain that has ultimately carried him to success. Throughout his life, he has displayed a strategic and proactive use of BrainPower, whether it is taming the emotional centers of the brain such as the amygdala to stay cool-headed when fans get a little rowdy or his ability to calibrate his anterior cingulate and frontal-parietal attention network to toggle his focus between playing Lucille and singing (he never does both at once). Of course, he doesn't walk around thinking about the turning of gears within his neural machinery, and we certainly don't expect you to either. It's enough to know that the brain is constantly revising itself throughout a lifetime, regardless of whether or not you have a plan to take control of how it operates. We believe you'll get better results if you take charge of the process and learn to cultivate the cognitive habits of a Winner's Brain like those relied upon by B. B. King and so many others you've met in this book.

So, ask yourself: Now that you've read this book, do you have more information about your brain and what it takes to achieve your goals and realize your dreams? Is your Opportunity Radar dialed in? Is your Goal Laser turned up to high? Is your Effort Accelerator at full throttle? Is your Talent Meter fully charged? Is your Optimal Risk Gauge set to go? And have you grasped the potential to shape how your brain functions? If you can answer yes to any of these questions, then you've picked up a few tricks of this cutting-edge trade and you are more of a Winner than you were before you cracked the binding of this book.

And you didn't have to run into a burning building to do it.

References

Introduction

Weissman, D. H., et al., *The neural bases of momentary lapses in attention.* Nature Neuroscience, 2006, 9(7): 971–978.

Gusnard, D. A., et al., *Persistence and brain circuitry.* Proceedings of the National Academy of Sciences, 2002, **100**(6): 3479–3484.

Maguire, E. A., et al., *Navigation-related structural change in the hippocampi of taxi drivers.* Proceedings of the National Academy of Sciences, 2000, **97**(8): 4398–4403.

Chapter 1. A Quick Brain Tour

Phelan, J., *Who is Rodin's Thinker?* ArtCyclopedia, August 2001, http://www.artcyclopedia.com/feature-2001-08.html.

Chapter 2. The Amazing History of Modern Neuroscience

Harlow, J. M., *Recovery from the passage of an iron bar through the head.* Publications of the Massachusetts Medical Society, 1868, **2**: 327–346.

Broca, P. *Remarques sur le siège de la faculté du langage articulé, suivies d'une observation d'aphémie (perte de la parole).* Bulletin de la Société Anatomique, 1861, **6**: 330–357. English translation by C. D. Green available at: http://psychclassics.yorku.ca/Broca/aphemie-e.htm.

Wernicke, C. *Der aphasische Symptomencomplex: eine psychologische Studie auf anatomischer Basis.* In Wernicke's Works on Aphasia: A Sourcebook and Review (G. H. Eggert, ed.), 1874/1977, 91–145. The Hague: Mouton Publishers.

Scoville, W. B., and B. Milner, *Loss of recent memory after bilateral hippocampal lesions.* Journal of Neurology, Neurosurgery, and Psychiatry, 1957, 20:11–21.

Berger H., *Ueber das Elek- trenkephalogramm des Menschen.* Archiv für Psychiatrie und Nervenkrankheiten, 1929, 87: 527–570. English translation: P. Gloor, *Hans Berger on the electroencephalogram of man,* EEG Clinical Neurophysiology, 1969, 28 (Suppl.):1–36.

Chapter 3. BrainPower Tools

Cunningham, W. A., C. L. Raye, and M. K. Johnson, *Neural correlates of evaluation associated with promotion and prevention regulatory focus.* Cognitive Affective and Behavioral Neuroscience, 2005, 5(2): 202–211.

Tom, S. M., et al., *The neural basis of loss aversion in decision-making under risk.* Science, 2007, 315: 515–518.

Jaramillo, F., et al., *Getting the job done: the moderating role of initiative on the relationsip between intrinsic motivation and adaptive selling.* Journal of Personal Selling and Sales Managment, 2007, 27: 59–74.

Gusnard, D. A., et al., *Persistence and brain circuitry.* Proceedings of the National Academy of Sciences, 2002, 100(6): 3479–3484.

Eddington, K. M., et al., *Neural correlates of promotion and prevention goal activation: an fMRI study using an idiographic approach.* Journal of Cognitive Neuroscience, 2007, 19(7): 1152–1162.

D'Argembeau, A., et al., *Modulation of medial prefrontal and inferior parietal cortices when thinking about past, present, and future selves.* Social Neuroscience, 2009, Sept. 21: 1–14.

Kruger, J., and D. Dunning, *Unskilled and unaware of it: how difficulties in recognizing one's own incompetence lead to inflated self-assessments.* Journal of Personality and Social Psychology, 1999, **77**(6): 1121–1134.

Win Factor #1. Self-Awareness

Di Pellegrino, G., L. Fadiga, L. Fogassi, V. Gallese, and G. Rizzolatti, *Understanding motor events: A neurophysiological study.* Experimental Brain Research, 1992, **91**:176–180.

Northhoff, G. and F. Bermpohl, *Cortical Midline structures and the self.* Trends in Cognitive Sciences, 2004, **8**(3): 102–107.

Schyns, P. G., L. S. Petro, and M. L. Smith, *Transmission of facial expressions of emotion co-evolved with their efficient decoding in the brain: behavioral and brain evidence.* PLoS one, 2009, **4**(5): 1–16.

Hudson, E. *Snow Bodies: One Woman's Life on the Streets.* 2004. Edmonton: NeWest Press.

Ersner-Hershfield, H., G. E. Wimmer, and B. Knutson, *Saving for the future self: neural measures of future self-continuity predict temporal discounting.* Social, Cognitive, and Affective Neuroscience, 2009, **4**: 85–92.

Lieberman, M. D., et al., *Putting feelings into words: affect labeling disrupts amygdala activity in response to affective stimuli.* Psychological Science, 2007, **18**(5): 421–428.

Goldberg, II, M. Harel, and R. Malach, *When the brain loses its self: prefrontal inactivation during sensorimotor processing.* Neuron, 2006, **50**(2): 329–339.

Dunning, D., K. Johnson, J. Ehrlinger, and J. Kruger. *Why people fail to recognize their own incompetence.* Current Directions in Psychological Science, 2003, **12**(3): 83–87.

Win Factor #2. Motivation

Eddington, K. M., et al., *Neural correlates of promotion and prevention of goal activation: an fMRI study using an idiographic approach.* Journal of Cognitive Neuroscience, 2007, 19(7):1152–1162.

Gusnard, D. A., et al., *Persistence and brain circuitry.* Proceedings of the National Academy of Sciences, 2002, 100(6): 3479–3484.

De Martino, B., D. Kumaran, B. Seymour, and R. J. Dolan, *Frames, biases, and rational decision-making in the human brain.* Science. 2006, 313(5787): 684–687.

Csíkszentmihályi, M. *Flow: The Psychology of Optimal Experience.* 1991. New York: Harper Collins.

Limb, C. J. and A. R. Braun, *Neural substrates of spontaneous musical performance: fMRI study of jazz improvisation.* PLoS One, 2008, 3(2): e1679.

Amabile, T. M., *Effects of external evaluation on artistic creativity.* Journal of Personality and Social Psychology, 1979, 37(2): 221–233.

Volpp, K. G., et al., *A randomized controlled trial of financial incentives for smoking cessation.* New England Journal of Medicine, 2009, 360: 699–709.

Steel, P. *The nature of procrastination.* Psychological Bulletin, 2007, 133(1): 65–94.

McCrea, S. M., et al., *Construal level and procrastination.* Psychological Science, 2009, 19(12): 1308–1314.

Elliot, A. J., et al., *Color and psychological functioning: the effect of red on performance attainment.* Journal of Experimental Psychology: General, 2007, 136(1): 154–168.

Win Factor #3. Focus

James W. *Principles of Psychology.* 1890. New York: Henry Holt and Co.

Weissman, D. H., et al., *The neural bases of momentary lapses in attention.* Nature Neuroscience, 2006, 9(7): 971–978.

Raymond, J. E., K. L. Shapiro, and K. M. Arnell, *Temporary Suppression of visual processing in an RSVP Task: an attentional blink?* Journal of Experimental Psychology: Human Perception and Performance, 1992, 18(3): 849–860.

Fisher, R. *Is advertising flogging a dead horse?* New Scientist, 2005, 2531: 40–41.

Most, S. B., et al., *Attentional rubbernecking: cognitive control and personality in emotion-induced blindness.* Psychonomic Bulletin and Review, 2005, 12(4): 654–661.

Mack, A., and I. Rock, *Inattentional Blindness.* 1998. Cambridge, MA: MIT Press.

Slagter, H. A., et al., *Mental training affects distribution of limited brain resources.* PLoS Biology, 2007, 5(6): 1228–1235.

Jha, A. P., J. Krompinger, and M. J. Baime, *Mindfulness training modifies subsystems of attention.* Cognitive, Affective, and Behavioral Neuroscience, 2007, 7(2): 109–119.

Tang, Y.-Y., et al., *Short-term meditation training improves attention and self-regulation.* Proceedings of the National Academy of Sciences, 2007, 104(43): 17152–17156.

Green, C. S., and D. Bavelier, *Action video game modifies visual selective attention.* Nature, 2003, 423: 534–537.

Eriksen, C. W., and J. D. St. James, *Visual attention within and around the field of focal attention: a zoom lens model.* Perception and Psychophysics, 1986, 40(4): 225–240.

Orr, J. M. and D. H. Weissman, *Anterior cingulate cortex makes 2 contributions to minimizing distraction.* Cerebral Cortex, 2009, 19(3): 703–711.

Smilek, D., et al., *Relax! Cognitive strategy influences visual search.* Visual Cognition, 2006, 14: 543–564.

Limb, C. J. and A. R. Braun, *Neural substrates of spontaneous musical performance: fMRI study of jazz improvisation.* PLoS One, 2008, 3(2): e1679.

Win Factor #4. Emotional Balance

Yerkes, R. M., and J. D. Dodson, *The relation of strength of stimulus to rapidity of habit-formation.* Journal of Comparative Neurology and Psychology, 1908, 18: 459–482.

Ochsner, K. N., et al., *Reflecting upon feelings: an fMRI study of Neural systems supporting the attribution of emotion to self and other.* Journal of Cognitive Neuroscience, 2004, 16(10): 1746–1772.

Boehm, J. K., and S. Lyubomirsky, *Does happiness promote career success?* Journal of Career Assessment, 2008, 16(1): 101–116.

Gross, James J. (ed.), *Handbook of emotion regulation.* 2007. New York: Guilford Press.

Ochsner, K. N., and J. J. Gross, *The cognitive control of emotion.* Trends in Cognitive Sciences, 2005, 9(5): 242–249.

Banks, S. J., et al., *Amygdala-frontal connectivity during emotion regulation.* Social, Cognitive, and Affective Neuroscience, 2007, 29: 1–10.

Richards, J. M. and J. J. Gross, *Emotion regulation and memory: the cognitive costs of keeping one's cool.* Journal of Personal and Social Psychology, 2000, 79(3): 410–424.

Win Factor #5. Memory

Bar, M., *The Proactive brain: using analogies and associations to generate predictions.* Trends in Cognitive Sciences, 2007, 11(7): 280–289.

Schött, B. H., et al., *The dopaminergic midbrian participates in human episodic memory formation: evidence from genetic imaging.* Journal of Neuroscience, 2006, **26**(5): 1407–1417.

Kensinger E. A., and D. L. Schacter, *Memory and emotion.* In M. Lewis, J. M. Haviland-Jones, and L. F. Barrett (eds.), The Handbook of Emotion, 2008, 3rd Edition. New York: Guilford.

Kondo, Y., et al., *Changes in brain activation associated with use of memory strategy: a functional MRI study.* NeuroImage, 2005, **24**: 1154–1163.

Bor, D., and A. M. Owen, *A common prefrontal-parietal network for mnemonic and mathematical recoding strategies within working memory.* Cerebral Cortex, 2007, **17**(4): 778–786.

Poldrack, R., et al., *The neural correlates of motor skill automaticity.* Journal of Neuroscience, 2005, **25**(22): 5356–5364.

Kensinger, E. A., and D. L. Schacter, *When the Red Sox shocked the Yankees: comparing negative and positive memories.* Psychonomic Bulletin and Review, 2006, **13**(5): 757–763.

Brown, R., and J. Kulik, *Flashbulb memories.* Cognition, 1977, **5**: 73–99.

Cook, S. W., Z. Mitchell, and S. Goldin-Meadow, *Gesturing makes learning last.* Cognition, 2008, **106**(2): 1047–1058.

Wylie, G. R., J. J. Foxe, and T. L. Taylor, *Forgetting as an active process: an fMRI investiation of item-method-directed forgetting.* Cerebral Cortex, 2008, **18**(3): 670–682.

Win Factor #6. Resilience

Waugh, C. E., et al., *The neural correlates of trail resilience when anticipating and recovering from threat.* Social, Cognitive, and Affective Neuroscience, 2008, **3**: 322–332.

Caria, A., et al., *Regulation of anterior insular cortex activity using real-time fMRI.* Neuroimage, 2007, **35**(3): 1238–46.

Pizzagalli, D. A., et al., *Resting anterior cingulate activity and abnormal responses to errors in subjects with elevated depressive symptoms: a 128-channel EEG study.* Human Brain Mapping, 2006, 27(3): 185–201.

Rotter, J. B. *Social learning and clinical psychology,* 1954. New York: Prentice-Hall.

Robinson, M. D., *Gassing, braking, and self-regulating: error self-regulation, well-being, and goal-related processes.* Journal of Experimental Social Psychology, 2007, 43: 1–16.

Banks, S. J., et al., *Amygdala-frontal connectivity during emotion regulation.* Social, Cognitive, and Affective Neuroscience, 2007,. 29: 1–10.

Zhong, C., A. Dijksterhuis, and A. D. Galinsky, *The Merits of Unconscious Thought in Creativity.* Psychological Science, 2008, 19(9): 912–918.

Frankenstein, U. N., et al., *Distraction modulates anterior cingulate gyrus activations during the cold pressor test.* Neuroimage, 2001, 14(4): 827–836.

Win Factor #7. Adaptability

Kelly, S., *The sat-nav v. cabbie challenge.* BBC-Click, Dec. 14, 2007, http://news.bbc.co.uk/2/hi/programmes/click_online/7143897.stm.

Maguire, E.A., et al., *Navigation-related structual change in the hippocampi of taxi drivers.* Proceedings of the National Academy of Sciences, 2000, 97(8): 4398–4403.

Sluming, V., et al., *Broca's area supports enhanced visuospatial cognition in orchestral musicians.* Journal of Neuroscience, 2007, 27(14): 3306–3799.

Aydin, K., et al., *Increased gray matter density in the parietal cortex of mathematicians: a voxel-based morphometry study.* American Journal of Neuroradiology, 2007, 28: 1859–1864.

Raue, U., et al., *Improvements in whole muscle and myocellular function are limited with high-intensity resistance training in octogenarian women.* Journal of Applied Physiology, 2009.

Lazar, S. W., et al., *Meditation experiece is associated with increased cortical thickness.* Neuroreport, 2005, 16(17): 1893–1897.

Siegle, G. J., C. S. Carter, and M. E. Thase, *Use of fMRI to predict recovery from unipolar depression with cognitive behavior therapy.* American Journal of Psychiatry, 2006, 136: 735–738.

Classen, J . Focal hand dystonia—a disorder of neuroplasticity? Brain, 2003, 126: 2571–2572.

Candia, V., et al., *Effective behavioral treatment of focal hand dystonia in musicians alters somatosensory cortical organization.* Proceedings of the National Academy of Sciences, 2003, 100(13): 7942–7946.

Win Factor #8. Brain Care

Hertzog, C., et al., *Enrichment effects on adult cognitive development.* Psychological Science in the Public Interest, 2009, 9(1): 1–65.

Oliff, H. S., et al., *Exercise-induced regulation of brain-derived neurotrophic factor (BDNF) transcripts in the rat hippocampus.* Molecular Brain Research, 1998, 61: 147–153.

Larson, E. B., et al., *Exercise is associated with reduced risk for incident dementia among persons 65 years of age and older.* Annals of Internal Medicine, 2006, 144(2): 73–82.

Erickson K. I., et al., *Aerobic fitness is associated with hippocampal volume in elderly humans.* Hippocampus, 2009, 19(10): 1030–1039.

Perez, J. A., et al., *A new role for FGF2 as an endogenous inhibitor of anxiety.* Journal of Neuroscience, 2009, 29(19): 6387–6379.

Geda Y. E., et al., *Cognitive activities are associated with decreased risk of mild cognitive impairment: The Mayo Clinic population-based study of aging.* Paper presented at the 61st Annual Meeting of the American Academy of Neurology, 2009, Seattle.

Small, G. W., et al., *Your brain on Google: patterns of cerebral activation during Internet searching.* American Journal of Geriatric Psychiatry, 2009, 17(2): 116–126.

Yehuda, S., S. Rabinovitz, and D. I. Mostofsky, *Essential fatty acids and the brain: from infancy to aging.* Neurobiology of Aging, 2005, **26S**: S98–S102.

Dangour A., et al. *Fish consumption and cognitive function among older people in the UK: baseline data from the OPAL study.* Journal of Nutrition, Health and Aging, 2009, 13: 198–202.

Chan, A., V. Graves, and T. B. Shea, *Apple juice concentrate maintains acetylcholine levels following dietary compromise.* Journal of Alzheimer's Disease, 2006, 9: 287.

Williams, C. M., et al., *Blueberry-induced changes in spatial working memory correlate with changes in hippocampal CREB phosphorylation and brain-derived neurotrophic factor (BDNF) levels.* Free Radical Biology and Medicine, 2008, 45: 295–305.

Yoo, S.-S., et al., *The human emotional brain without sleep—a prefrontal amygdala disconnect.* Current Biology, 2007, 17(20): R877–R878.

Sterpenich, V., et al., *Sleep-related hippocampo-cortical interplay during emotional memory recollection.* PLoS Biology, 2007, 4(11): 2709–2722.

Lazar S. W., G. Bush, R. L. Gollub, G. L. Fricchione, G. Khalsa, and H. Benson. *Functional brain mapping of the relaxation response and meditation.* NeuroReport, 2000, 11: 1581–1585.

Wagner, U., et al., *Sleep inspires insight.* Nature, 2004, **427**(6972): 352–355.

Ruxton, C. H. S., *The impact of caffeine on mood, cognitive function, performance and hydration: a review of benefits and risks.* Nutrition, 2008, 33: 15–25.

Epilogue

Limb, C. J. and A. R. Braun, *Neural substrates of spontaneous musical performance: fMRI study of jazz improvisation.* PLoS One, 2008, 3(2): e1679.

Acknowledgments

Although we are experts in our various fields — both of which are related to the study of the brain—we understand so much more about neuroscience and success now than when we began *The Winner's Brain*. And yes, we've also learned much about what we don't know, too. As time goes on, we're confident that evidence for the connection between the brain and achievement will become even stronger.

Throughout the researching and writing of this book, we used our Opportunity Radars to connect with, and learn from, a multitude of people who we consider part of *The Winner's Brain* team—we can't thank them enough:

Julie Silver, M.D., Chief Editor of Books at Harvard Health Publications, who conceived the idea for *The Winner's Brain,* assembled our author team, and tirelessly carries the banner of encouragement.

Tony Komaroff, M.D., Editor-in-Chief of Harvard Health Publications, whose own passion is to get information to people so they can live healthier lives. We thank him for making our mission easier through his leadership.

Linda Konner, our literary agent, who provided rock solid wisdom, humor, a heart of gold, and GPS-like ability to hunt down a New York City taxi.

Katie McHugh, our Perseus editor, who shepherded this book with patience and grace. Every author should have the experience of being guided by such a thoughtful and insightful person.

The entire Perseus and Da Capo teams, who have made us feel like family and have selflessly invested in the message of *The Winner's Brain* on behalf of us and their devoted readers.

Karly Neath, Melena Vinski and Angele Larocque, who provided important assistance, and the remaining members of the Fenske lab at the University of Guelph for their sheer enthusiasm and useful suggestions.

Moshe Bar, Ph.D., Director of the Cognitive Neuroscience Laboratory at the A.A. Martinos Center for Biomedical Imaging at Massachusetts General Hospital and Harvard Medical School, who has been unbelievably generous with his time and expertise and who provided valuable comments on various drafts of the book.

Bruce Rosen, M.D., Ph.D, Director of the Martinos Center, along with Mary Foley, Larry White, and Linda Butler, who generously provided time and resources to arrange brain scans of the entire Winner's Brain Team.

There are more than fifty Winner's Brains from all walks of life who openly and frankly shared their fascinating life journeys with us so we could relate them to you, our readers. Their stories have brought the brain science to life and allow all of us to revel in their accomplishments. We offer sincere appreciation to each and every one of them, including the many noted researchers and scientists who generously provided their knowledge, opinions and cutting-edge research.

Finally, we would like to thank our wonderful families for taking up the slack and giving us the copious amounts of time and support that were needed to write this book. Thanks and love to: Carolynne, Karen, and Jay, our spouses and most patient supporters. And the same love to: Skylar, Grant, Nathan and Jake, our children and biggest fans.

Index

About the Authors

JEFF BROWN, PsyD, ABPP, is a board-certified clinical and cognitive-behavioral psychologist on faculty in the Department of Psychiatry at Harvard Medical School and a Clinical Associate at McLean Hospital, Harvard's largest psychiatric facility. He is a member of the Association for Applied Sport Psychology, the American Psychological Association, the United States Olympic Committee's Registry of Psychologists, and is a Fellow of the Academies of Clinical Psychology and Behavioral Psychology.

Dr. Brown is considered a pioneer in bringing sports psychology to the masses. In 2002, he became the first psychologist to serve on the Boston Marathon medical team. In addition, in 2008 he joined the Chicago Marathon and Houston Marathon medical teams as team psychologist. Dr. Brown is also the author of *The Competitive Edge*. He lives and practices in Boston. To learn more about Dr. Brown's clinical and consulting practice, visit his Website at www.DrJeffBrown.com.

MARK FENSKE, PhD, a former research fellow and faculty member at Harvard Medical School, is an Assistant Professor (Neuroscience & Applied Cognitive Science) in the Department of Psychology at the University of Guelph. As a specialist in cognitive and affective neuroscience, his research combines neuroimaging with behavioral studies to reveal how attention and emotion influence cognitive performance.

Dr. Fenske serves on the editorial boards for the journals *Emotion* and *Psychological Research,* and has been a reviewer for nearly two dozen professional publications, including *Journal of Cognitive Neuroscience, Cerebral Cortex, Cognitive Brain Research,* and *Neuropsychologia.* In addition, he was selected in 2009 to serve on the Committee of Experts in Psychology, Psychiatry and Cognitive Neuroscience by the Canada Foundation for Innovation. He lives in Guelph, Ontario. Additional information about Dr. Fenske's research can be found at his laboratory Website at www.FenskeLab.ca.

LIZ NEPORENT is a Senior Vice President at Wellness 360, a health writer and author of several best-selling health titles. She is currently a contributor and Health Coach for AOL.com, and she also contributes to dozens of national publications, including *The New York Times, The New York Daily News, Shape, Fitness, Men's Health,* and others. She lives in New York. Visit her Website at www.w360.com.

Made in the USA
San Bernardino, CA
05 May 2014